HISTORIC COTTAGES
OF GLEN LAKE

Barbara Siepker

For Bruce and Bonnie,

For your enjoyment of the history

5/25/2012

❊

Historic Cottages
of Glen Lake

Barbara Siepker
Dietrich Floeter, photography

Lou Heiser, illustrations

Leelanau Press, 2008
Glen Arbor, MI 49636

This is the second publication of the Leelanau Press, a nonprofit publisher, whose mission
is to publish Leelanau County writers and artists. It was founded by Barbara and Frank
Siepker. P.O. Box 115, Glen Arbor, Michigan 49636, Siepker@aol.com, 1-800-303-6956

Locating these cottages and learning their stories has been by word-of-mouth and
interviews. There are more known and unknown that we are sorry not to have been able to
include. We apologize for any incorrect information. We learn through mistakes and expect
to stand corrected.

Siepker, Barbara and Floeter, Dietrich
Historic Cottages of Glen Lake
History of summer cottages and resort life 1900-1950s on Glen Lake, Michigan. Over fifty
cottages, exteriors and interiors, were photographed by Floeter using large format black
and white cameras. Illustrations by Lou Heiser. Old maps, old photographs and postcards
illustrate the historical text. 300 photos and illustrations. Printed in duotone.

Library of Congress Control Number: 2007907178
ISBN: 978-0-9742068-0-6
Cover and book design by Saxon Design, Inc.
Manufactured, printed and bound in in the United States of America
First Printing 2008

Dedication

This book is dedicated to the historic Glen Lake cottages. They provided years of comfort and joy, as well as background and substance for many loving memories and stories. We thank the current owners of the cottages portrayed in this book for their willing cooperation, access to the interiors, for sharing the cottages' histories and family photographs. We appreciated this rare opportunity and ask that their privacy be respected.

It is also dedicated to the Lydia Green Cottage which was included in the initial fifteen cottages that were photographed and on display at the Leelanau Historical Society in 2005. This phase was supported by the 2004 Edmund F. Ball Fellowship. The impetus for this book began at that show and has grown to include thirty-five more cottages.

Lydia Green, a teacher from Cadillac, built this quaint one-bedroom cottage with knotty pine interior in 1936 to rent. It continued as a rental after it was purchased by the Carr family from Midland in 1957. It sold in 2005 and was torn down to make room for a new home.

We hope this book will increase appreciation and recognition of the importance of these historic cottages in the lives of their owners and the community. It is a tribute

that these often simple and primitive structures maintain a centering place in a family's lore and history. These once vibrant dwellings are now endangered and disappearing from our landscape as lakefront prices, property taxes and renovation costs increase, especially when ownership is transferred. We are ever grateful to those who care about and share a commitment to preserving these historic summer cottages which are an important part of the history of Glen Lake.

Robert and Roland DeWitt Cottage, a Bellaire pre-cut log cabin, 1959

Contents

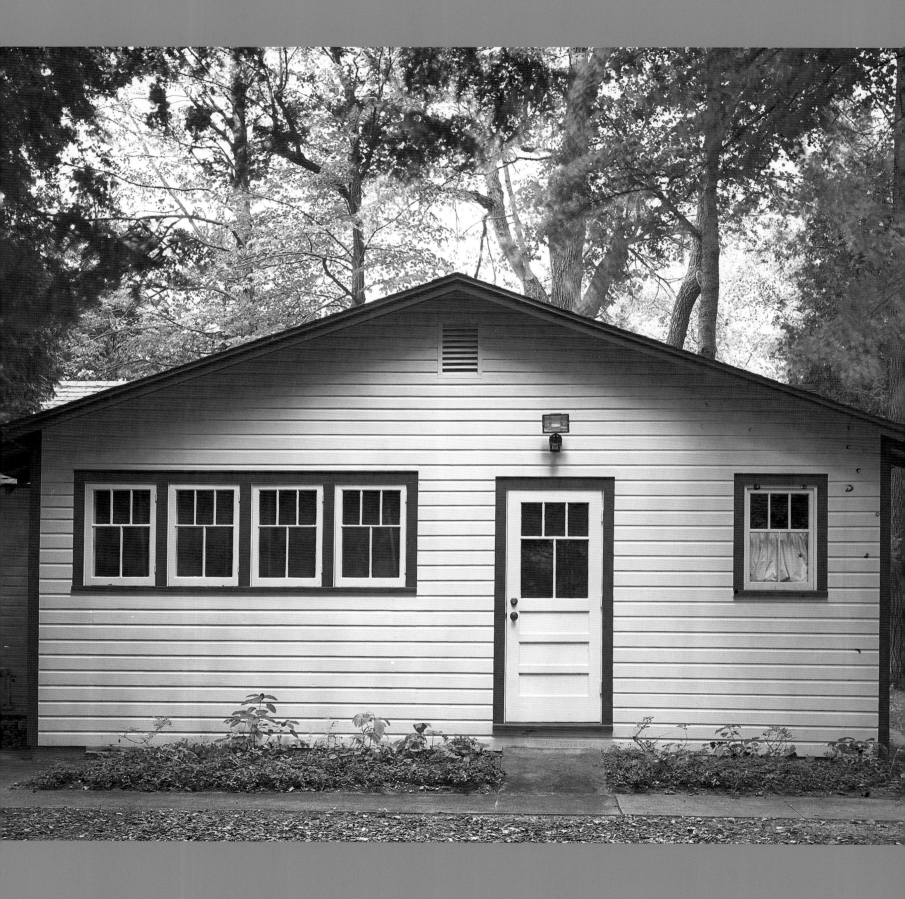

PREFACE

The idea and impetus for this project began in 2000, out of love for the cottages, built during the heyday of summer resort life on Glen Lake, that were disappearing from the landscape. Dietrich Floeter, architectural photographer, was enlisted to shoot a number of the remaining cottages. Both exterior and interior images were photographed using the black and white view cameras that were available during the early resort era. When it was difficult to capture an exterior shot, drawings were rendered by Lou Heiser, a nationally recognized architect-artist who summers on Glen Lake. In some cases, vintage photographs supply unique images. History of each cottage's life is conveyed in anecdotal fashion, gleaned from interviews with current and past owners. As presented in total and with a little nostalgic imagination, the hope is that they adequately convey the ambiance and nuances of the Glen Lake cottage experience which was so endeared by it participants.

Originally fifteen cottages were photographed and exhibited in 2005 at the Leelanau Historical Museum, a project funded by the Edmund F. Ball Fellowship. Thirty-seven cottages have been documented and photographed since that time and are the nucleus of this book. A historic cottage is defined as having been built in the first half of the twentieth century. As was the owner's custom, all are referred to as cottages, no matter how small or large. Locating the old cottages has been mainly by word-of-mouth and makes no claim as to be complete. The ones selected met the criteria that their integrity had not been compromised during remodeling and additions. Purposefully a range of sizes and styles, from simple rental to grand architect-designed cottages, are included. Some are log kit and pre-cut kit cottages.

Cottage architecture in this area changed following World War II, as did vacation patterns. These cottages reflect a simpler, more primitive life-style sought by the early vacationers. Tenting and primitive bathroom and kitchen facilities were accepted as part of the ambiance of the life-style. Privacy within the cottage was non-existent, even with curtains and partitions. This fostered family intimacy and closeness not always available in their larger, often servant-filled homes. Summers on the lake were peaceful and idyllic, filled with recreational activity and often with social lives that seemingly replicated those they'd left at home, but likely with more freedom and less pressure. Other families sought refuge from that life and closely guarded the privacy that a remote lake cottage afforded.

Thirty-three of the cottages are no longer owned by original families and in a few cases information about early owners is sketchy, at best. Six of the cottages remain in the original family; in some the fourth generations now own it. As we spent time getting to know each cottage, we found that each one had a unique story to tell about its origin, its architecture, its owners, its neighbors and family experiences summering on Glen Lake. Our intent is to honor the past and to appreciate the love and care that has been given to these cottages for over 100 years.

U.S. Coast Guard
Light House

North Manitou

North Manitou Shoals Li...

Latitude – 45 Degrees North
Halfway Line Between North Pole and Equator

Submarine Cable

Pyramid Point
Elevation 400 Feet above
Lake Michigan – Graveyard
of many lake vessels – High
sand bluff –

Sand Dune

Manitou Passage
Used by most ore freighters
and boats of all types between
Chicago and the Straits
of Mackinac –

Andreson
Lake

Pyro...

M22

Bass

Sleeping Bear Bay

Lake
Area
360 a.

Sleeping Bear Sand Dune
One of the largest migrating dunes
in the World – Length 6 miles –
Average width 2 miles. Height
above Lake Michigan 350 to 400
Feet. This dune has been a famous
landmark for lake navigators
for over 100 years –
Sleeping Bear Pinnacle
The highest point on the dune.
Height above Lake Michigan –
600 feet –

Sleeping   Bear Point

U.S. Coast Guard
Station
Glen Haven
Old Pier

Leelanau Schools
Crystal River
Outlet to
Glen Lake

Glen Arbor

M22

M22

671

Miller's
Hill–Fine
View
300 feet above
Glen Lake

M109

Glen
Lake

Fisher
Lakes

671

Glen Lake
Elevation above
Sea Level – 598 Feet.

Total Area 7680 Acres

616

M22

The Narrows

Burdickville
Settled in 1859
by William
Burdick

616

North Bar Lake
Area – 80 acres

M109

Site of
Old Catholic
Church – 1867
Old
Benzonia
Trail

Lookout
300 ft. above
lake

614

South Bar Lake
Area 160 Acres

Glen Lake is considered by many authorities
to be one of the most beautiful lakes in
the world. Its great depth (250–300 feet)
gives its surface a hue of deep turquoise
blue and emerald green. The brilliant
yellow of Sleeping Bear Sand Dune
is reflected in its ever changing surface.

Empire Village –
Named for schooner
which sank here
in the early
days –
Population
300 –

M22

M76

M76

Empire Bluffs
Elevation
400 ft.

Wallis
Lake

Neustad
Lake

M22

Leelanau County
Organized in 1862–1863. 11 townships –
Area – 206,762 acres. Population (1942) 8423 –
Over 100 miles of Lake Michigan shore-
line. Lumbering was main industry
in the early days. Farming, fishing,
and fruit growing are main occupations.
The county is a well known resort area
with 25 inland lakes within its borders.
There are many beautiful scenic views. --

–Drawn by–
Frederick W. Dickinson
"The Studio"
Art shop on Glen Lake
Empire, Michigan

INTRODUCTION

COTTAGE LIFE

The family lake cottage is steeped in shared experience and nostalgia that seems to defy logical explanation. Perhaps, it is because vacations lie outside of the realm of daily pressures and routine. What is not to love about being without care, free to enjoy family and friends in a gorgeous surrounding? Time spent at the lake is a gift that provides special memories of fun-filled days and keeps family traditions alive. As the years pass, it seems that these simpler times become even more appreciated and cherished.

Cottage memories are visual and sensory experiences, the joy of the first glimpse of the lake each summer and the delightful shiver of the first dip into the lake. Others remember the smell as they entered the cottage or the aroma of grandmother's pies baking. Among the first memories of one of the Addoms twins is the beauty of the boathouse interior where they stayed on Glen Lake when she was two years old. The sting of sand blown by strong winds across the dunes and the pounds of sand gathered in cuffs and shoes tracked into the cottage are all part of summer life.

The lake cottage was the sustaining entity and staging point for the summer lake vacation. Birthdays, weddings, honeymoons, and other important family functions were celebrated here. Sometimes it was the one time the whole family was able to gather, with siblings overlapping their stays. Intergenerational traditions continue so that cousins and grandchildren experience similar happy times. For families scattered across the country and the world, the lake cottage was the one consistent "home."

In truth, the lake vacation has changed much since World War II. It is far less common for mothers and children to stay for the entire summer. In some families, cottage ownership has been divided, necessitating shorter stays so that each family owner can have time at the lake. Even so, the memory of halcyon days at the lake cottage remains an important part of family lore.

YOU ARE HERE

Glen Lake lies in the southwest corner of Leelanau County in northwest Lower Michigan. Leelanau County is actually a peninsula which extends northward into Lake Michigan. A Michigander understands the geographical locater by pointing to the top half of the little finger on an upraised hand. Leelanau, referred to as "The Land of Delight", has 105 miles of Lake Michigan shoreline, 33 inland lakes, pristine beaches, deep woodlands, cherry orchards, farmland and vineyards. The bodies of water moderate the weather extremes. Glen Lake lies between the small towns of Glen Arbor and Empire, surrounded by the Sleeping Bear Dunes. When the national park was proposed in the 1960s, there was strong local opposition. Summer residents banded together with the local community and fought a bitter battle with the government. Although they lost in 1976, most now agree the 71,000 acre national park has successfully preserved their beloved dunes and natural areas.

Glen Lake sits partially within the borders of the Sleeping Bear Dunes National Lakeshore and encompasses over 6,000 acres. A bridge spans the area called the Narrows making it appear as two lakes. The smaller basin is often referred to as Little Glen and is used in this book to help distinguish cottage locations. The lake's 17 miles of shoreline is surrounded by high forested hills with sandy soils that were formed during the glacial era. A thin ring of coveted private property and cottages hugs the shoreline.

Glen Lake is a beautiful, spring-fed glacier formed lake. In summer the sun reflects off its sandy bottom and through its crystal clear waters. Rich turquoise blues and greens shimmer in the sunlight and its range of colors are

likened to the Caribbean waters. In some areas, up to several hundred yards of knee-deep water circles the shore of the lake. This band reflects a much lighter hue than the deep center where the lake reaches a depth of 130 feet. John McCormick first arrived at Glen Lake in the dark from Cincinnati as a young teen. As he walked to see the lake first thing in the morning, his feet became wet. He was used to the brown water of southern Ohio and had walked right into the lake without realizing it. He had never seen such clear water.

At the western end of Little Glen stands the Dune Climb. Hills surround the lake and provide a scenic backdrop to the beauty of the lake from every side. Alligator Hill, with its prominent alligator shape offers the same silhouette from both sides of the lake. Glen Lake, the Dune Climb, Alligator Hill, Lake Michigan and the Manitou Islands can all be seen from Inspiration Point on the south side of the lake. These beloved landmarks are protected from future development as they are all within the park's boundaries. Lakefront property owners love their sunrises and sunsets and proclaim their particular view as "the best around the lake." The views, in fact, are all beautiful and restorative to the soul.

First settlers

The area's first summer residents were nomadic Native Americans who left their winter quarters further south and traveled north by large dugout canoes along the Lake Michigan shoreline. With the opening of the Erie Canal, schooner and ship traffic increased dramatically on Lake Michigan. Chicago was one of the world's busiest ports. Up to 100 ships a day could be seen coming through the Manitou Passage around 1900. This was the favored shipping route passing between the mainland and the two Manitou Islands.

Cordwood for ship's boilers was sold all along Lake Michigan's shores. The Manitou Islands, stopping points for ships to make repairs and load up with provisions and cordwood, were settled before Leelanau County. Northern European immigrants began moving to the mainland in the 1850s and established homesteads. Farms and later orchards were carved out of the once heavily forested land. The Dorseys, Tobins, Dunns, and Rays established farms through governmental homestead claims along the shores of Glen Lake. They farmed the land for crops and their livestock would cool off and drink water from the lake. Potatoes were an abundant crop in Port Oneida just north of Glen Lake.

Soon lumber camps were established, largely to ship lumber to Chicago. Trees were cut in the woods all winter and skidded down iced chutes in hills to the shores of Glen Lake. Logs were stacked and then transported to the sawmills in the spring. By the end of the 1800s, all first growth trees and even some of the second-growth had been felled. Nomadic lumbermen moved on to new locations. Fortunately, some landowners were conservation-oriented and replanted the forests they then selectively cut. Local entrepreneurs looked to other sources of income. They planted apples, cherries, peaches and pears that grew well in the area's temperate sandy soils. They also began to encourage summer tourism in concert with the ship and railroad lines.

Charles McCarty purchased land and platted Glen Haven in 1857. He built a sawmill, a dock and the Sleeping Bear Inn. McCarty sold out to Northern Transportation Company in 1868 and moved away. D.H. Day, who worked for Northern Transportation, was assigned to this area and decided to remain. He purchased the steamship line and the town of Glen Haven. Day was an entrepreneur and continued to purchase land around the lakes. His lumbering operation had two tug boats and a barge that hauled logs across Glen Lake to the sawmill at the west end of Little Glen near the base of the Dune Climb. As early as 1909, Day established an electrical plant in Glen Haven which lighted his skating and curling rink. Around the lake, electricity was not established until the late 1920s. More progressive farms had Delco battery systems in the barns to provide power for the farm machinery. A few early cottages rigged gravity-fed water tanks and at least one was run by a "one lunger" engine.

A FINE PLACE TO BE

In the 1890s, paralleling a similar trend nationwide, businessmen from Midwestern cities took up the sport of fishing. Fishermen were first lured to the crystal clear inland lakes and streams of northern Michigan by stories of large and abundant fish. The men camped and fished the Platte and Betsie Rivers. They reveled in the natural beauty of the area and the healthy life it offered and soon returned with their families to vacation.

By the 1900s, more summer visitors began coming to flee the heat and conditions of crowded cities. Newly industrialized cities were not pleasant places to be during the heat of summers and one's health was at risk for asthma and hay fever. Stories about the clean air, cool summer breezes and beautiful scenery enticed them to northern Michigan, urged on by doctors' recommendations to leave the cities during the summer. Nature and outdoor activities provided a fun and healthy summer lifestyle. Brochures touting the area began to be distributed by steamship lines in the large cities to encourage tourism.

THE WORD WAS OUT

Descriptions of this glorious lake filled tourist promotional materials. Glen Lake was labeled "The Most Beautiful Lake in Michigan" on a postcard and on a circa 1928 Glen Lake map identifying cottage owners and area attractions. These were produced at the time of the opening of a grand vacation wonderland, the Day Forest Estates on Alligator Hill. The Glen Haven dock welcome sign announced the Glen Lake Region as the "Como of America" and advertised resorts, cottages, and land for sale. On July 31, 1926, a *Traverse City Record-Eagle* article titled "Glen Lake the Most Beautiful Lake in Nation" made the statement "Glen Lake is one of the five most beautiful lakes in the world." This statement was attributed to Columbia University Professor Laphan, a *National Geographic Magazine* writer. Proud summer residents shared this boast in their home communities. However, later they used as their reference a 1934 *National Geographic Magazine* article even though the author Maynard Owen Williams stated that he could find no written evidence for this declaration. In his article about touring around the great lakes, Williams did state that he had never seen a more beautiful lake. The rumor persisted as it matched closely held convictions.

Visitors were most often smitten upon first encounter. In no time, the lake worked its magic and often commitment and dedication followed. There are surprisingly similar stories heard about how people first fell in love with Glen Lake. Oral interviews confirmed the supposition that newcomers were usually introduced to this remote lake by family and friends. It many cases, esteemed community leaders influenced friends to join them. Thus, there were large number of families from Hinsdale, Illinois, Toledo, Ohio, Detroit and Lansing, Michigan. Vacationing here had the added benefit of companionship with friends and relatives in an informal setting surrounded by nature.

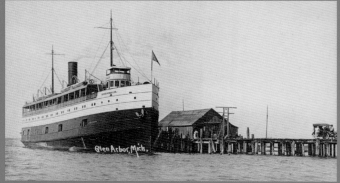

Glen Haven dock with *Missouri*   *(Whiteside Family Collection)*

Bill and Edith Burrow in horse-drawn buggy
(Lund-Atkinson Family Collection)

HOW THEY ARRIVED

Early summer visitors, mostly from Chicago, came by ship to Glen Haven or Glen Arbor and remained all summer. One way tickets cost $5. With steamer trunks piled high on resort-operated horse drawn wagons, families were delivered to lakeside resorts that offered tenting or tiny primitive cottages.

Women and children most often came for the entire summer and the men commuted on weekends. The men left Chicago Friday evening after work, played cards, slept in staterooms and arrived Saturday morning. They had much to fit into their one and a half days here. They returned Sunday night and arrived in time for work Monday morning. The ships they took were the *Puritan, Missouri, Illinois* and the newer, better appointed *Manitou.* There was a always a festive gathering in Glen Haven Sunday afternoons as parting families were joined by local people on their weekly Sunday outings.

Alternative transportation was by train to Traverse City where a Pullman sleeping car was dropped off in the middle of the night so as not to interrupt sleeping. The resort staff or family would pick them up in Traverse City or Cedar, if they had booked a connecting train. Somewhat later, cars were driven to Glen Lake and left for the summer, with some of the family still traveling by train or ship. Other families reported driving fully loaded cars, running boards piled high with needed goods and household animals. In the 1920s, the trips from Detroit and Chicago took two to three days on gravel roads that turned to sand

Atkinson family on the road, circa 1920s *(Lund-Atkinson Family Collection)*

Clark family out for a horse and wagon ride in the early 1900s
(Beaird Family Collection)

Casparis family, early 1940s   *(Casparis Family Collection)*

and dirt at Cadillac. Frequent tire and car repairs were a part of the adventure. Families would stay in tourist rooms overnight and Clare, south of Cadillac, was a favored spot to stay at the hotel.

EARLY YEARS ON THE LAKE

For a period of time in the early 1900s, lumbering operations and summer tourism around Glen Lake existed simultaneously. D.H. Day's sawmill on the west shore of Little Glen was still in operation. Tug boats pulled log rafts from around the lake to the mill, and a narrow gauge railroad transported the cut wood from the mill to the Glen Haven dock. The tugs and the train were known to ferry a few passengers, as well. The highlight of the summer was the annual Old Settlers Picnic in Burdickville which honored the early settlers. At one time there was a dance pavillion with a calliope. Day ferried people to the picnic on his barge.

Nessen's Glen Arbor Lumber Company had a sawmill and dock on the northeast side of Glen Lake between 1899 and 1907. Nessen also had a dock in Burdickville. A narrow gauge railroad transported the logs from Lake Street to the dock in Glen Arbor near the Sylvan Inn. The engine was sold to Day when Nessen ceased operations but slab wood from the lumber yard continued washing ashore for many years.

Marie Ambrosius rowing her aunt and friend while watching Dorsey's cattle tow a dock, circa early 1910 *(Baad-Johnson Family Collection)*

Helen towing barge loaded with logs on rail cars, circa late 1910s
(Empire Area History Museum)

D.H. Day's tug near the Narrows returning to the mill, early 1900s
(Jill Cheney Collection)

A log raft being towed to D.H. Day's sawmill   *(Peppler Family Collection)*

Teal built by Frank Fisher *(Empire Area History Museum)*

Johnson family at Old Settlers Picnic *(Dunn Family Collection)*

D.H. Day's engine *(Vintage Views Archives)*

Breaking up camp in 1896 at A.R. Clark's near the Narrows
(Empire Area History Museum)

Frank Fisher had built the *Teal* to tow logs to his mill on the Crystal River which remained in operation until the early 1930s. He also used the *Teal* to take passengers on pleasure excursions and fishing trips.

The local farmers and businessmen established mutually satisfying relationships with the summer residents. The farms provided food, lodging and services. Many interviewees vividly described Herman Brammer's ice delivery, how the ice was cut in the winter on Glen Lake, packed with sawdust and stored in icehouses around the lake. Brammer later sold garden produce when refrigerators replaced the iceboxes. Jack Barratt delivered milk from the Burfiend Farm in Port Oneida and John Dorsey had a milk delivery route on Little Glen. John's mother Josephine ran a laundry on their farm that serviced Gregory's Tonawathya, Ocker's and several cottage owners. Frank Fisher's son Eugene ran a boat livery between 1909 and 1920. For the next six years it lists him as running an auto livery and taxicabs. By the late 1930s, Gene Fisher had built *Miss Leelanau* and for about ten years ran fishing and scenic excursions for hire from his cottages on the east side of Glen Lake. (*Miss Leelanau* is pictured on the Fisher Cottages page, pg. 152.)

Living was simple and quite primitive. There were several small tenting communities of groups of friends. One was Kingfisher's Camp on Fisher Lake and another nearby on the east shore of Glen Lake at Sewama Heights. There was no indoor plumbing or running water and cooking was done over fires or on wood cookstoves. Improbable by today's standards, these early vacationers recreated in the standard dress of the day: long dresses, dress shirts and even ties. Their bathing suits, looking more like dress clothes, were made of itchy wool that never seemed to dry out. Resorts with limited sleeping room capacity provided tents, or visitors brought their own. As new owners purchased land, they often tented on it for many years before building and then during cottage construction. But there were no complaints, only devotion to the wonderful days spent on Glen Lake.

Where they stayed

By the early 1900s, there were six resorts around Glen Lake listed in three different tourist brochures. Little Glen had three: Kenwood, Cold Springs and Cedar Springs and Glen Lake had three: Tonawathya, Ray's and Atkinson's.

Kenwood Resort

In 1895, early settlers Henry C. and Anna (Tobin) King began Kenwood Resort on their farm on the south shore of Little Glen. Anna's parents, Richard and Ellen, had a homestead claim that bordered the Dorsey's property and extended from Kenwood east to the Narrows. The Tobins and Dorseys owned most of the south shore of Little Glen. The Kings built an eight-room cottage annex for guests who took their meals in the King's home. Overflow guests tented on the property. They had a tennis court and an active waterfront. The Glenmere post office opened in 1905 at the King's resort, but it was later moved to Richard Tobin's store near the narrows after Mrs. King died in 1918, just after the last of the summer guests left. The resort was then closed as she had been running it alone since her husband passed away in 1902.

Cold Springs Resort

Cold Springs Resort was a very large three-story frame building to the east of the King's and was built by John Bidleman who was married to a Tobin. The property had flowing springs thought to be good for one's health. A large two-story porch encircled the entire building and the help lived on the third floor. It served all meals and had spacious rooms. By the 1920s, it had became Ocker's Resort. It was renamed Glen Lake Manor by its new owners in the 1950s. Although wonderful postcards exist, less history is known about this resort as it has been closed for many years. The only restaurant on Glen Lake opened a few years ago in the renovated building now called the Manor.

The Frank Dillon family vacationed at Kenwood Resort. Frank's friend Walker Jamar took these photographs beginning in 1905
(Dillon Family Collection)

17

Cold Springs Resort with car on road

Cold Springs Resort taken by Walker Jamar

Cedar Springs Resort

Cedar Springs Resort on the north shore of Little Glen consisted of a large lodge and cottages by the lake. It was run by S.S. Burke and had a Glenmere post office address. The *Leelanau County: The Land of Delight* 1924 brochure listed it as Verbeck's Resort. As it burned down shortly after that, it is rare to find anyone who still remembers its existence. John Dorsey and Dottie Lanham remember their fathers taking them over there to see the charred remains.

Ocker's Resort

Cedar Springs Resort

Ray's Resort   *(Vintage View Archives)*

Atkinson's pond and sawmill   *(Lund-Atkinson Family Collection)*

Atkinson's for-hire launch in Burdickville *(Lund-Atkinson Family Collection)*

Ray's Resort

Welby C. Ray built Ray's Resort close to the Narrows on the southwest shore of Glen Lake—likely about the same time he sold the family farm to the Gregorys. Welby was married to Elizabeth (Diodge) who was often called Lizzie. She became a teacher and taught in Glen Arbor and was also a writer published serially in a few national magazines. She died in 1922 and their son Max Milton and his wife Nellie (Hebert) took over running the resort. Ray's Resort was a white building with a front porch which held two swings and chairs. A spacious, comfortable lounge held sofas, chairs and a piano. There was a large dining room and a kitchen on the first floor and five bedrooms on the second with a bath on each end. Nellie did all of the cooking and ran the laundry behind the kitchen. The property also had a shuffleboard court and a two-story bunkhouse for their two or three hired girls. Several cottages were located on the north side of the property and one to the south, which was sold to the George and Marge Howard in the mid-1930s when they established Howard's Edgewater Resort. After the Rays sold the resort in the mid-1940s to William Gross, it became known as Glen Lodge. In 1979 it was sold to Gerald and Janice Peer. The original lodge was taken down in 1993 and replaced.

Atkinson's Resort

Atkinson's Resort and Trout Ponds was on the south shore of Glen Lake, east of Burdickville Hill, in small area called DeGrauville, named after the original owners of the property, DeGrau and Parrant in 1883. Located across the road from Glen Lake on Little Indian Brook Trout Pond, it had a working sawmill and farm. Years before, the Native Americans had dammed the spring-fed creek creating a pond to keep the fish alive in the winter. The good fishing at Atkinson's appealed to fishermen. The resort was likely begun by J.C. Lardie (married to a Tobin) in 1891 and then sold to Albrecht in 1901. Beginning in 1907, Asher M. and Marilla Atkinson owned it for 15 to 20 years and ran the resort which had six large rooms upstairs and a large dining room and living room downstairs. Atkinson had a launch

Atkinson's Resort   (Lund-Atkinson Family Collection)

for hire that he moored on Glen Lake in Burdickville. The pond and creek were later named for John Hatlem who purchased the property in the 1930s. The Inn burned down in the early 1940s. The Hatlems rebuilt a smaller home in the same location and rented out cottages. Atkinson's daughter Edith was married to Chicago policeman Bill Burrow. One day, while building his cottage, he brought a friend to the Hatlem's home and asked Mrs. Hatlem if he could pay her to fix them a meal. She had a reputation for being a good cook and obliged the two men. That was the beginning of the Hatlem's restaurant which became sought after for her full-course meals served at four seatings a day for just $1.25. In the 1930s, just to the east of Hatlems was the popular dinner club, the Green Dragon.

Platform tent at Gregory's Tonawathya   (Whiteside Family Collection)

Tonawathya

The resort which plays the most important role in this book was located on the west shore of Glen Lake. Tonawathya, also referred to as Gregory's, was owned by Frank A. (Jr.) and Anna Gregory. They had heard about Glen Lake from avid fishermen Homer Frank and Charles Field. Mr. Gregory was comptroller at National Lead Company (which later became the Dutch Boy Paint Company) in Chicago and Mr. Field was his boss. As it had been recommended that both the Gregorys seek clean air and relaxation for their health, they decided to visit the area. In the 1890s, the Gregorys rented a room in Welby C. and Lizzie Ray's farmhouse, on land owned by his parents, George C. and Sarah (French) Ray. In the 1850s, the senior Rays homesteaded 100 acres and established an apple orchard of 1000 trees with Welby. The Gregorys began purchasing the Ray farm in 1901 and continued to acquire additional adjacent acreage. Along with the resort they named Tonawathya, they continued to operate the farm, orchard and had dairy cows, pigs, chickens and a vegetable garden. Early on, overflow guests tented on the property.

Tonawathya soon earned recognition as a formal resort which provided all meals. Mealtime was announced by bells. The first bell rang one half hour before mealtime and anyone not seated by the second bell was not served. Dress attire was required for dinner. Popular menu items were repeated during the week. Sunday night featured lobster bisque. At midnight on Saturday nights Welsh rarebit was served with beer and on Wednesday evenings, picnics were held, as the help had the night off.

The inn contained ten upstairs rooms. Downstairs there was a large living area, formal dining room, back kitchen, music room, library and Mrs. Gregory's office with a bay window. The Gregorys lived in a two-room suite upstairs. Their help, John August and Hilda Johnson, came with them from Chicago for the summers. Sometime before the 1920s, the Gregorys began to build cottages that they rented out to returning families who continued to take all of their meals at the inn.

Carl A. and Lucy (Andresen) Oleson maintained the property for the Gregorys from the early 1920s until Carl's death in 1944. They had a home behind the Rookery, a two-story building, where the eight girls lived who cleaned and worked in the kitchen. They slept on the sleeping porches and dressed in the dressing rooms behind. There were three turnstiles that held the animals in two pastures. A cow path went behind the cottages to the south leading to the second pasture where the cows grazed during the day. A rose arbor was built early on that led from the road to the long front porch and entrance to the inn.

Resort activities included swimming, fishing, boating, tennis, shuffleboard, horseshoes, croquet, Ping-Pong and picnic outings. Guests returned by invitation only. They came from Ohio, Indiana and Illinois, with a large number from Hinsdale, Illinois. The Gregorys began to sell their cottages as well as vacant land to previous renters who, having fallen in love with Glen Lake, wished to have cottages of their own. Twelve of the cottages photographed in this book were a part of Gregory's original property: Evelyn's, Worthington, Warren-Senter, Dunbar-Batchelder-Williams, Hench-Symonds, Wilson, Collings-Dunscombe, Raines, Fetzer, Burr, Barton, and Rea-Whiteside.

The Gregorys owned Tonawathya for nearly 50 years. In 1947 at age 82, their health was failing so they sold to Asa H. and Edna W. Case of Benzonia, Michigan, and Alfred S. and Catharine W. Oskamp of Glen Ellyn, Illinois. Several years later the Cases sold to Albert Wrisley who operated Cedar Lodge in Northport. Wrisley changed the name to Old Orchard Inn and ran it for some time. The property with nine cottages, caretaker's cottage and the Inn was sold to Katherine (Hench) Whitney, Scott and Helen (Hench) Jones of Hinsdale, Illinois, and Kane and Elizabeth Zelle of Springfield, Illinois. The Wrisleys ran it for them for a short while as did several other couples until a consultant advised that the Inn should be razed as it was not feasible to renovate it. They closed the resort and had the Inn burned in a controlled fire department train-

Tonawathya Inn *(Fornowski-Kroeber Family Collection)*

Children on turnstile *(Whiteside Family Collection)*

Anna Gregory, 1910
(Fornowski-Kroeber Family Collection)

Glen Eden Hotel and Cottages

(Vintage View Archives)

ing session, circa 1970. The owners planned on developing the property but the U.S. government purchased much of it for the Sleeping Bear National Lakeshore. The remaining portion was sold. Three new homes stand where the Inn once did and grapes are now cultivated in part of what was the old orchard.

By the early 1920s, there were three additional resorts on Glen Lake: Glen Eden Hotel, Krull's Resort and Dunn's Farm Resort.

Glen Eden Hotel

Dr. Clara Belle Hooper, a widow from Toledo, Ohio, was an osteopathic doctor. Around 1920 she purchased Fisher Point and established the Glen Eden Hotel, a health facility whose daily regimen for improved health was good food, fresh air, and exercise. Several cottages were added and meals were taken at the main lodge. She sold it to Pete and Tina Wrisley, brother to Albert, about ten years later. Dick and Lois Henry purchased it in 1964 and ran the resort until 1981 when Dan and Jan Semple took over its operation. It was sold and taken down in 2004.

Krull's Resort

By 1920, Christian and Louise (Peppler) Krull had purchased the Nessen's Glen Arbor Lumber Company including the mill and lumberjacks cottages at the end of Lake Street on the north shore of Glen Lake. Chris had come from Detroit to work in the orchards and would sail daily to and from work on Miller Hill. Krull's began resort operations out of the brown main lodge on Lake Street which they named Krull's Exclusive Glen Lake Resort. Meals were served for guests staying in the upstairs rooms and the lumberjacks cottages which had been moved to the beach. Louise's family was German and had been bakers. She was a good cook and prepared all the meals. The main meal was served at 1:00 p.m. On laundry day, when the kitchen was turned into a laundry room, lunch was soup. After World War II, their son Christian married Theola "Teddy" Field, Harford Field's daughter. They began Glen

Craft Marina and became a Century boat dealer. They also ran a resort, adding more cottages designed by her father and built by Chris and Harford, Jr.

Dunn's Farm Resort

John and Bridget Dunn homesteaded on the east shore of Glen Lake in 1864. They originally came from Ireland and had arrived in Glen Arbor via Canada with their oxen and just enough supplies to establish their farm. Around the turn of the century, their son James and his wife Katherine (Doran) took over running the farm which had swamp land along the lakeshore and was considered the back side of the farm. This changed as lakefront property became desirable to increasing numbers of summer residents. Katherine's father was a wheelwright in Glen Haven. She sewed beautifully and was a wonderful cook. Her granddaughter, Patricia (Johnson) Dutmers, believes the resort started one day early in the 1920s when someone stopped by and asked if they could have dinner. They began to take in summer guests, and in 1925 added onto the big house, as the family called it, and built four cottages without kitchens.

The resort provided a "real vacation" with guests taking meals in the dining room wing of the house. There were seven upstairs bedrooms for guests. The *Calcutt* and *Boyd Cottages* were named after the people who rented them. The others were named *Yellow* and the *New Cottage*. Three spring-fed creeks run through the property and feed into Glen Lake. Whatever was fresh from the garden was served at the three daily meals at 8:30 a.m., 12:30 and 6:00 p.m., announced by a warning bell and then the serving bell. Men dressed in jackets for dinner. Mrs. Dunn cooked the meals, assisted by her daughter Sarah (Johnson). Three or four girls waited tables and local boys washed the dishes. Mrs. Sickles walked daily from Miller Hill to run the laundry. The Cooks, Schillings, Brydges, and Andrews, were among the first families to come to the resort. They all built cottages to the south on land purchased from the Dunns. Some owners continued to come daily for dinner.

Dunn's Farm Inn and Barn *(Vintage View Archives)*

Croquet in front of Orchard Cottage at Dunn's Farm

Dunn's Farm, looking north to the big house, laundry and playground

Margaret's Cottage at Dunn's Farm *(Dunn Family Collection)*

Dunn's Dining Room   *(Dunn Family Collection)*

Sarah Johnson in front of sugar bush   *(Dunn Family Collection)*

The Kramps family, who summered across the lake north of the Narrows, came regularly for Sunday chicken dinners, served with warm biscuits, gravy and homemade ice cream for dessert.

The land continued to be farmed and summer families living nearby on the shore would have their children row the boat over for milk and eggs. The farm produced most of the food for the resort. Sarah had a cherished sugar bush. She boiled down the sap in the spring to make maple syrup. All of the family worked at the resort.

This family resort could accommodate 50 to 60 people. Both Mrs. Johnson and Mrs. Dutmers felt close to their guests saying "We're like one big family." There was not much need to advertise as guests came through word-of-mouth from Detroit, Chicago, Ohio and New York staying from a couple of weeks to a month, some for the entire summer. Guests swam, boated, fished, played croquet, tennis and shuffleboard. Evenings, board games and cards were played along with nightly gatherings around the piano and singing. They also donned costumes and performed masquerade skits for each other. Later, another four cottages were built: *North, Cabin, Orchard* and *Margaret's Cottage.*

The resort stopped serving food in the 1950s and at that time kitchens were added to the cottages. Grandchildren and even great-grandchildren of original vacationers continue to come to stay and visit at Dunn's Farm. Many have purchased and built cottages around Glen Lake and have become summer residents. The Watsons have been coming to Dunn's Farm for over 80 years and the Duckwalls for nearly 50 years. Some of the original cottages are now owned by family members and have been renovated, moved or taken down. Unlike most of the other resorts, Dunn's Farm has always been owned and operated by the family and has the honor of being the only resort on Glen Lake still in existence. It has been awarded the Michigan Centennial Farm designation.

These early resorts played an important role in the development of the area as they provided lodging for many families who would later build their own cottages either on the resort's property or nearby on the lake. The resorts also accommodated many who continued as renters. While the relaxing setting of the lake provided a welcome respite from the constraints of life back home, the decorum of the day was strictly enforced. Resort life offered something for everyone, companionship, good food and activities to fill the days. They were carefree vacations that left their own set of nostalgic memories.

COTTAGES WERE BUILT

The early Glen Lake cottages were simple in design, layout and structure. Ten of these cottages were designed by prominent architects from the families' home communities. As was more often the case, cottages were designed without architects. Some were planned by a family member who envisioned what it should look like. Some designs were chosen from magazines or books that published plans, others were builder's plans. In the early cottages there were sleeping porches with beds or cots instead of bedrooms. Later they were enclosed and windows added. The smallest cottages had a simple open plan with small bedrooms off a central room. Many began without bedroom doors. Curtains were hung to offer some privacy. When closets were added, they were also without doors.

Porches facing the lake were open or screened to take advantage of the healthy air and capture cooling breezes. These sitting porches were the center of cottage life. They often had cots, beds, gliders or swings and were preferred places to sleep, listening to the sounds of the night. Meals were often taken on the porch, games played and guests entertained. The outdoors was part of cottage life, almost an extension of the cottage. Daily life flowed inside and out, one almost didn't notice a door until it banged.

Cottage furniture was simple and sometimes handmade. Furnishings were most often metal beds with metal box springs, bunk beds, built-in bunks, chairs and tables, couches and a few small tables. Some were furnished with new furniture that was shipped here, others outfitted with discarded furniture brought from home. Log furniture, especially beds, was built by the builders of the cottages, such as Joe Gersh. When cottages changed hands, they came furnished. Larger, grander cottages had spacious bedrooms, closets, bedroom doors and guest books that recorded cottage life. One guest book enumerated each type of linen in the cottage, listing both good and worn towels, a reminder that both were necessary. Cottages managed to collect a trove of nature's treasures. Hardly a cottage stands that does not have a piece of driftwood, Petoskey stone, pine cone, feather, shell or collection of pretty stones.

Bill Dotterweich's parents first brought him to Glen Lake as a baby in 1936. They rented a cottage from Dr. Lake who was also from Jackson, Michigan. Bill describes Glen Lake cottages as not being fancy, with outhouses, hand water pumps, kerosene cook stoves, iceboxes and a potbellied stove in the center of the room. As there was no garbage delivery, trash was buried outdoors. Renters were told to leave the cottages "broom clean" for the next guests. Even though Bill and Peggy Dotterweich purchased a new home in 1997, their children still prefer to stay in their old cottage on the property.

HOW THEY WERE BUILT

The early cottages were often built with the timber felled as the property was cleared. Some lumber was hand-hewn on site and others sawed at local saw mills. The latter showed the circular saw markings. There were several saw mills operating during varying time-frames: D.H. Day, Frank Fisher, Verlin Stearns, Novotny Brothers, Aylsworth and Empire Lumber. Some owners had lumber sent from their home communities that arrived by ship at Glen Haven or by truck to the property. The pre-cut kit homes, shipped mostly from Michigan companies, usually came with everything needed to construct and to furnish a cottage. There were no local hardware stores. Traverse City

Frank Fisher's sawmill located on the Crystal River near Fisher Lake
(Jill Cheney Collection)

Mrs. Myra Hans and two of the Novotny brothers at the sawmill
(Santucci-Hans Family Collection)

Verlin Stearn's sawmill, late1930s   *(Swierad Family Collection)*

stores, Hannah Lay Lumber and Brown Lumber, paid $50 a year in 1930 to have billboards in Glen Arbor.

Early log cottages were generally full-log with notched corners and constructed of cedar or tamarack, the preferred woods. These logs were cut in the inland swamps the season before, so that they were seasoned by the time of construction. Later there were also cedar log kits, manufactured by the Michigan-based Braun and Bellaire companies, which were half-logs assembled vertically. These kits also arrived on site with all the materials and instructions for assembly.

The majority of the cottages were simple wood-framed structures with siding on the exterior and a low pitched gabled roof. Often the exterior wall also served as the interior wall with the studs exposed. Roof supports were often left exposed under the eaves providing an unfinished cottage look. Prevalent birch logs were sometimes used for porch railings and as accent trim; more rarely it was used in interiors. Inside, the dividing walls for rooms reached only ceiling height, leaving the open roof rafters exposed. Over the years, ceilings and wood walls were added, providing the interiors with a more closed, finished space. Local woods, tongue-and-groove knotty cedar and pine, were most often used along with beaded board which was originally natural but later painted. When wood was not used, the material most often used was Celotex, the predecessor to drywall. Celotex was composed of natural cane fiber and came in an unfinished surface or a buff-colored surface which could be painted. This material provided some insulation.

In the early days, with no building inspectors or building standards, construction and additions were not what we would term today as being "up to code." There were even stories about shacks made out of orange crates. Foundations were primitive. Some were simply posts, likely cedar, used at the corners and center wall supports. One cottage had corner posts set on top of rocks, another had one support resting on the stump of a felled tree. Support beams were hand hewed or even full logs in early construction. It was not unusual for lumber and other materials discarded from one cottage to be re-used for another cottage. Structures such as boathouses, schools and churches were moved and formed the shell of the cottage. Eventually, these could no longer be recognized as the original structure. Over the years, many changes occurred to the original structures. Often cobbled together, the additions make for unique floor plans and unusual traffic patterns. These changes accommodated the desire for kitchens, bathrooms, needed storage, laundry rooms and additional bedrooms for growing families. Some owners added basements, crawl spaces or Michigan basements.

Living on a spring-fed lake, owners dealt with water. Springs are known to appear spontaneously where they had not been before. Wells are the main source of water.

Water tables are high and cottages were often located on top of filled lowland and swamps. Moisture beneath cottages caused major structural damage and contributed to mold and mildew. Replacement of damaged support beams and floors was difficult with inadequate crawl spaces. Early septic systems were primitive, sometimes just holes dug in the ground or dry wells.

Some cottages had brick or stone fireplaces originally, and some had them added later. Fireplaces helped keep the morning and night chill out of the cottage. Sometimes they were the only source of heat during a cold spell and cottagers huddled around the fire wrapped in blankets. Fieldstone, left behind when the glaciers retreated, was abundant and favored for its aesthetic appearance. The stone was gathered locally and stories abound about the hunting and gathering operations and the best building method. Children were often employed in this work, especially when Glen Lake stones were gathered. Stones were also found along the Lake Michigan shore. The majority came from farmers' fields, left at the edge of the fields that had been cleared. Later, gravel quarries in nearby Maple City provided a supply of fieldstone.

Stonemasons' names were often not remembered. The workers were obtained by the builders and many were Native Americans. Some were northern European immigrants who brought their craft with them and lived in the inland communities of Lake Leelanau, Cedar and Maple City. Often masters in their craft, no two stone fireplaces and chimneys are alike. The styles vary dramatically, but pride in their construction are evident. The chimney designs varied from straight to tapered with all round (full) stone or a combination of cut and round placed in patterns. Stone size and the amount of exposed mortar vary considerably in each cottage. Stones were cut or split by hand with a skilled blow to its surface. A few families recalled the stonemason either had to be released from jail for some minor infraction or had to be located in a local bar to get a job completed. Some contractors also could be found at Art's Tavern.

COTTAGE CARE

Maintaining the cottage was an important part of living on the lake. Over the years, owners developed a list of cottage maintenance and functioning procedures that would instruct family members or renters and would be passed along to new owners. For closing, there were a set of instructions for draining pipes, fixtures and water tanks so that pipes would not freeze and burst during the harsh winter months. Spring opening had another list. Cottagers are known for collecting fleets of every type of boat, floatation device and accessory. Docks, swim platforms, and boat lifts need to be put in and taken out every season. Boats and motors had their own list of maintenance and storage procedures. Even cottage signs and mailboxes needed to be brought in to protect them from the winter snow.

Every cottage infra-structure is distinctive. Passing along the stories and traditions for caring for it is like giving a gift to the new owners. For many years, there were no pre-purchase inspections of the mechanics of the cottages. Sometimes cottages were purchased sight unseen. When such a list was not provided, a call would need to be made to the previous owner for instructions such as to where the water heater or fuse box was located. When Charles Wallace purchased his cottage on the east shore, it came with a long handwritten letter of instruction. It had been gathered over the years and was lovingly shared by Margaret Bates whose family were the first owners of the cottage.

Maintenance chores became a part of the tradition of owning cottages and tended to be a self-appointed responsibility. It was a chance to arrive early and return late in the season. Weekends were devoted to the various opening and closing functions and friends and family had fun working together. Occasionally, there was even time for some fishing. However, final leave-taking at the end of the season was always tinged with sadness as families bid farewell to their beloved cottage, neighbors and summer memories.

Women's entertainment in the early 1900s at Gregory's Tonawathya Resort while the men worked in Chicago   *(Whiteside Family Collection)*

SUMMER FUN

Summertime was all about leisure and play. Adventures and activities first were organized by the early summer resorts that dotted the lake. Fun-filled days were spent hiking, picnicking, swimming, canoeing, sailing, playing tennis, shuffleboard, horseshoes, golf, croquet, and cards. At Tonawathya Resort, women worked on their handiwork together, read in hammocks and took evening strolls to the Narrows bridge which was a new attraction when it was re-constructed in 1905. The men fished or golfed and played horseshoes in the evening. Music played a central role and many social events included singing and playing instruments. A major source of entertainment at the resorts was skits and masquerade parties. With many of the men away during the week, the women dressed up and played the men's parts. Weekly dances included whole families.

Like other summer residents, Lillis Lanphier Lyon has wonderful memories of Glen Lake. She grew up feeling the area was her own personal playground. She observed that families seemed to stick together more when here than they did back home. The Glen Lake Yacht Club was the center of activity for the younger generation. Entire days and nights were spent hanging out together sailing, swimming and playing. Dune Climb excursions extended into the night with baseball games and capture-the-flag. Her father, Charles "Chick" Lanphier, an electrical engineer, loved wiring. He wired a speaker outside his children's bedroom, waking them up at three in the morning to come out and see Jupiter's moon rising. He built a hill-top observatory at the Leelanau School which still entertains summer visitors now in its new location on the beach.

The Henry Kraus family stayed at Tom House's *Maplecroft* at the recommendation of friend Andy Anderson from Akron, Ohio. Although they rented only three years, son Chuck's memories are vivid and compelled him to return years later with his family on what has turned into an eighteen-year tradition. At twelve years of age, he went out very early to fish, bringing back small fish to feed to the large pike in Baxter's fish tank. Chuck recalls the cottage they stayed in had a sailing vessel print above the fireplace. He also remembers waking to the sound of the percolator. It was a thrill to be invited to taste House's famous silver dollar pancakes.

Steve Senter wrote a touching ten-page tribute for his parents' fiftieth wedding anniversary celebrated at Glen Lake in 1993. It concluded with his heartfelt memories. "Glen Lake is the spiritual and emotional center of the place and heart-breakingly beautiful The color of the water is phenomenal, impossible to capture in painting, a combination of the reflection of the blue sky and the short, blue, light waves bouncing of the infinite H-two O's (sic) in the Lake" (and the sand bottom).

FISHING

Lake trout, which live in the deep waters, were the most common prey of fishermen. In the 1800s, they were called Mackinaw trout. Frank Fisher relates that in spring, when the trout were near the surface, his grandmother Charlotte Fisher would row her boat into Glen Lake and troll with minnows caught in the Crystal River. She caught Mackinaw trout using an improvised cotton line in the early 1900s. In the mid-1930s, Frank's father Eugene took several years to build a for-hire fishing and excursion boat. When it came time to deliver *Miss Leelanau* to Glen Lake, his brother Clint built a cradle on a trailer to pull the boat out of Lake Michigan. They motored the boat around the

Fishing from the Narrows' bridge   *(Whiteside Family Collection)*

Glen Lake from the "Top of the World" *(Zierk Family Collection)*

Mr. and Charles Mapes with pickerel in 1906 *(Empire Area History Museum)*

peninsula from Traverse City and took it out in Glen Arbor. It was delivered to Glen Lake just in time for the summer season. Fishing boats had large reels fixed to the stern. The reels first held copper line and later steel, with trolling bait on the end.

Fishing was good on Glen Lake and young boys, men and a few women fished daily. The back of a 1911 postcard reads, "We are catching them here that weigh 4 & 5 pounds. The boating and bathing we have here couldn't be beat." In later years, the lake was stocked with perch, bluegill, small-mouthed bass, northern pike and several varieties of trout. Dick Schilling remembers digging night crawlers and catching 25 to 30 perch before breakfast. They would drag two buckets behind the Chris-Craft to slow the boat down while trolling.

In the 1930s, Morry Baxter (Margaret Dunn) established a Standard service station on the corner in Burdickville where the lake was first spotted by vacationers arriving from Traverse City. He kept a large tank outside which contained a pike and sturgeon. This was a real attraction for young boys and sold lots of recommended lures.

Dr. C.G. Parnall purchased land on the Platte River and built this small cabin. He invited friends to fly fish and influenced several Springfield families to settle on Glen Lake. Dr. Parnall was from Ann Arbor and a college roommate of Charles Lanphier Patton. *(Lanphier Family Collection)*

Going fishing from Tonawathya *(Whiteside Family Collection)*

Casparis family on the Dune Climb *(Casparis Family Collection)*

Baily family picnic at Dunn's Farm *(Beaird Family Collection)*

Ladies on picnic table *(Atkinson–Lund Family Collection)*

Cornelius and Patricia (Johnson) on their horses at Dunn's Farm Resort *(Dunn Family Collection)*

Twenty-eight people for dinner at Clarks and Bailys near the Narrows, 1906 *(Empire Area History Museum)*

Jean Kilgore, center, on Gregory's dock 1930 *(Whiteside Family Collection)*

Sitting on Gregory's dock *(Whiteside Family Collection)*

Yacht Club diving platform *(Hench Family Collection)*

Clark and Baily families on the dock near the Narrows
(Empire Area History Museum)

SWIMMING

Docks and swim rafts were built all along the lake and were common centers for sitting and socializing, swimming, diving contests and tanning. Docks served the function of the front porch back home. Children's waterfront play was supervised along with leisurely visiting with adult friends. A few families had a tradition of swimming to their raft and back twice before breakfast.

Lanphier family at poplar beach in Glen Arbor *(Lanphier Family Collection)*

Gregory's busy dock *(Whiteside Family Collection)*

On Gregory's dock 1920s *(Hench Family Collection)*

SAILING

Glen Lake is a good sailing lake with a long history of sailing races. Even before the mid-1930s, there were a variety of large sailing boats on Glen Lake owned by sailors Fetzer, Wells, Danly and Kilgour. In the 1930s, races were informally organized by a youthful group and held two to three times a week, alternating weeks between Tonawathya Resort and Dunn's Farm Resort. Annual Regatta Days involved many ages and types of aquatic sports, and trophies were awarded. Organized largely by the Kilgours, they were advertised by flyer and were held at Tonawathya. This was before the Glen Lake Yacht Club was formally organized and had a clubhouse built in the early 1940s.

Beginning in the mid-1930s, Snipes became the popular class, as it did nationally, and as many as 21 were known on Glen Lake in the 1940s. These boats had a colorful main sail and jib and required two people to sail. They were built by Ray Greene in Toledo and brought to Glen Lake. Glen Lake's Fleet competed with some of ten other Michigan fleets. After World War II, Greene designed and sold fiberglass Rebel sailboats. In 1961 the District Three Championships were held on Glen Lake with 70 boats starting simultaneously.

Tom House built prams and had a colorful fleet of these dinghies. He gave lessons, held races and rented them from his resort on the east side of Glen Lake in the 1940s. Chuck Kraus learned the importance of orderly sailboat maintenance by observing Tom House. Nightly the boats were pulled up high on shore, the rudders stacked on a rack and the sails laid out to dry. House was Scottish and had served in the British Navy. When a newly built boat was launched, he played the bagpipes.

Chick Lanphier's motorized raft *Glen-Tiki*
(Lanphier Family Collection)

Glen Lake had one legendary swim raft that became mechanized. The Chick Lanphiers had one made that had six drum barrels that were mounted on shafts so that the raft could be rolled for easy launching. Within 24 hours, son Charles had mounted a five-horse powered motor. Eventually it held a railing, mast, umbrella, table, chairs, charcoal grill and a ship's bell. Boats tied up to the raft and hot dogs were served. Named *Glen-Tiki*, it was the envy of the lake, and made the papers in 1954 as the epitome of easy living.

Annual Regatta

of

Glen Lake Yacht Club

In front of Tonawathya and adjoining properties
on the west shore of Glen Lake.

August 12, 1939

YACHT RACE

Warning Gun	9:45 a. m.	Five Minute Gun	9:55 a. m
Starting Gun	10 a. m. E. S. T.		

Motor and Speed Boat Races

Start 2:00 p. m. E. S. T.

Second Race to be started immediately after the first is finished.
After the power boat races, all power boats will remain at anchor outside of the
swimming and canoe race courses until the swimming and canoe races are finished.

Swimming Races, Canoe Races and Tilting

The order in which these races shall be run is at the discretion of the judges; all contestants
shall be ready when their races are called. Prizes for all winners.

Row Boat Races

CANOE RACES

Ladies Doubles	50 yards, turn buoy and return
Mens Doubles	same
Mixed Doubles	same
Tilting Matches	Men and Mixed (Lady to Paddle)

SWIMMING RACES

Senior Girls over 16	50 yards straight-a-way	Boys *and* Girls under 10	15 yards straight-a-way
Junior Girls under 15	25	Relay 4 man teams	25
Senior Men over 16	50	Relay Fancy Dress	25
Junior Men under 15	25		

SURF BOARD RIDING

JUDGES: W. B. Burr, Wade Fetzer, J. L. Hench *and* Stuart Morgan
MARSHAL: Captain F. J. Marsh
ASSISTANT MARSHALS: Ray Greene, R. G. Peck, *and* Jerome K. Stock
TIMEKEEPERS: Charles Dunscombe, Carl Oleson, *and* Fred W. Adams

EVERYONE INVITED

Plenty of Room for Spectators.

COMMITTEE:

G. R. Barton	H. F. Field	F. A. Gregory	Geo. Johnson	H. B. Kilgour	R. C. Lanphier
W. M. MacLachlan		C. L. Patton		G. A. Schilling	Mrs. A. N. Tracy
	S. E. Dean			Harry E. Weese	

Masenich Printing Co., Traverse City, Mich

Annual Regatta, August 1939 *(Hench Family Collection*

Canoe tilting was one of the popular Regatta events *(Hench Family Collection)*

Motorboats

There were a number of early wood motorboats on the lake, including gas launches. For a couple of years in the early 1920s, Glen Arbor Township required gas-powered boats to be registered and charged $50 and $100 fees. Seven were registered in 1921 and eighteen in 1922. The early boats were often used for family motoring. Prior to there being a marina on Glen Lake, families had gas delivered to their cottages and stored it in drums. Several trips with gas cans had to be taken to their docks to pour enough fuel into the tanks.

George A. Schilling helped bring a Chris-Craft dealership to Harold Ralston's Marina on the Crystal River. The marina sold gas, did boat repairs and had a boathouse for boat storage. A few residents returned their Chris-Crafts nightly to Ralston's and had trouble maneuvering in the dark, as they would put off returning until as late as possible. Phil Krull built Glen Craft Marina after World War II. He was a Century Dealer.

Stories recall early competition between Schilling's and Fetzer's chauffer-driven Chris-Crafts—the first two on the lake. Later, boats were built that could go even faster for aquaplaning and skiing. Bud and Bob Byerly taught everyone on the northeast side of the lake to ski behind their big Chris-Craft or their super-fast little boat.

Will Whiteside in front of the excursion boat *Mae*
(Whiteside Family Collection)

Howard Tobin and sons launching A.R. Clark's *Helen* near the narrows, 1933 *(Erdmann Family Collection)*

Ralston's Boat Livery *(Lanphier Family Collection)*

Glen Lake boat *(Hench Family Collection)*

35

It was quiet much of the day on the lake and summer residents could hear the sounds of the boats. Sunny Brook's (Doepke) 1939 letter included the note that she had just heard a Chris-Craft starting up and that she loved hearing that sound. Kurt Wright recalls hearing the sound made by the partially submerged exhaust pipe and seeing the fore and aft lights at night. As his family did not own a boat, Nate Whiteside remembers being invited along on neighbor Fetzer's Chris-Craft.

Riding Dune Cars

In the late 1930s to late 1970s, one of the most popular area entertainment and tourist attraction was the Dune Rides. In 1935 Louis Warnes outfitted his car with a special motor and oversized balloon tires to enable him and his wife Marion (Day) to drive on the dunes. Soon he was begged to give rides to others which he did for $.25 each. It grew to an operation that eventually had four fleets of vehicles. In 1941 you could choose from a $.50 or $1 ride which began at the Warneses' Store, formerly Day's, in Glen Haven. Spectacular views were seen on this 15-mile course as drivers roared to the edge of a dune and suddenly stopped. The wild and scenic rides fluttered hearts, flipped

Touring the sand dunes   *(Atkinson-Lund Family Collection)*

stomachs, and were often accompanied by cowboy yowls. The moonlight trips were special. The Warneses provided coveted jobs for young locals and summering men who were proud dare-devils. The dune rides were discontinued when the national park purchased the property.

Golfing

There once were two golf courses on Glen Lake. The first was started in the early 1920s by a group of local and summer residents and was named Glen Lake Country Club. It was a fun and challenging nine-hole course that cost $1 to play and had caddies. It had a club house that held memorable Saturday night dances for all ages but closed about the time of World War II. William and Helen Peppler purchased the property in 1943 while he was serving overseas. For a time they lived in the clubhouse. They built Glen View Cottages on the golf course property advertising "There are no sneezes in Glen Lake breezes!"

A second sporty course opened in 1927. It was an 18-hole course designed by American Park Builders, a Chicago golf course development company with a national reputation, whose lead designer was Tom Bendelow. The golf course was one phase of Day Forest Estates, an exclusive summer resort planned by D.H. Day. The 2000-acre development had twelve miles of forested roads and 120 estate sites of five to thirty-five acres each. Day had visions of attracting a summer White House and a legislative bill for this possibility was to be proposed. Primarily located on Alligator Hill, it was designed to include a magnificent clubhouse, tennis club, polo field, horse trails, ski jump, and toboggan slide. Glen Lake frontage included an airfield and a small clubhouse with an elaborate stone and cement stairway that led to the beach and dock. Plans for the Lake Michigan side featured a larger beach clubhouse and dock for yachts. The only components actually built, however, were the stone entrance pillars still standing on M-22 and M-109, the golf course with starter's house and water tower, the airfield, and the stone stairway to the lake. Just

Day Estate stone entrance pillars *(Vintage Views Archives)*

View of Sleeping Bear Dunes from Day Estate Golf Course
(Vintage Views Arhives)

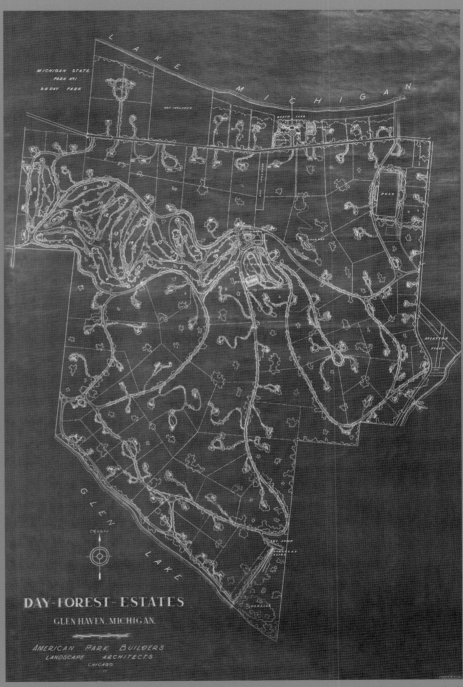

Day Forest Estates map *(The Cottage Book Shop)*

Glen Lake Country Club clubhouse   *(Peppler Family Collection)*

as the lots were opened for sale in 1929, the stock market crashed and no lots were ever sold. Day had died the year before in the spring of 1928.

The proposed development, however, brought widespread attention and new visitors to Glen Lake, which furthered community pride and the sale of Glen Lake waterfront lots. A number of grand cottages were built during this time frame. It was reported that the amount of luggage shipped to Glen Lake on ships and trains doubled in 1929. Those interviewed talked about hearing dynamite charges during the summer as stumps were being cleared for the Day Forest Estates roads and the golf course. While many played the course, none spoke of desiring to purchase as inexpensive lakefront lots were readily available. The airfield approach was treacherous as the runway began at the bluff where the Glen Lake Yacht Club is now. The Fetzer family recalls how a family member's approaching plane would circle the cottage to alert them to come and pick him up at the airfield. The water tower provided a competitive challenge to teenagers, especially after it was abandoned. After being sold three times, the tower was taken down for scrap in the mid-1970s.

This golf course was beautiful but a challenge to play. In 1939 Sunny Brooks (Doepke) wrote, "It's such a beautiful day here and was lovely playing golf with Helen (Hench) except I'm exhausted because you simply have to be a mountain goat to play on the course!" The course lasted into the 1940s. One family reported that their father drove them all over the fairways in his car. As he was not a very good driver, it was terrifying as they careened over the hills.

After a failed attempt in the late 1940s to get the state to purchase Day Forest Estates, a group of local and summer residents organized an effort to purchase it. It was priced at $100,000 and each interested party was to contribute $1000 in order to place an offer. The committee, consisting of Arthur S. Huey, Ralph H. Mueller, Dr. C. G. Parnall, Jack Rader and Marion H. Yoder, were not successful in placing an offer. Pierce Stocking, an experienced lumberman from Cadillac, Michigan, finally purchased it in 1949. He quickly built a sawmill and later added charcoal furnaces (still standing) for his operation at the base of Alligator Hill. He also owned much of the Sleeping Bear Dune and designed and built the original winding scenic drive with a stone water garden and picnic area at its entrance, just south of the Dune Climb. Stocking sold Day's original farm to contractor Don Lewis before he sold the Dune and Alligator Hill to the national park in 1976.

ESTABLISHING FAMILY TRADITIONS

Glen Lake leisure time was filled with playful teasing and wholesome, competitive outdoor activities. Even rainy days had their own traditions of curling up with a book, fires in the fireplaces and board games which are still kept on shelves. There was little time or chance for boredom or getting in trouble. If they weren't too tired after spending the entire day outdoors in the sun, families would often play games and cards in the evenings. Ann Haggarty Warren shared that in the 1940s they would play canasta for hours, and after a magnificent sunset seen from their cottage they would likely be ready for bed. If not, they heard their eighty year-old grandfather call from his room, "George, don't you think it's time for everybody to go to bed?"

Guest books hold clues to times well spent at the lake. In 1949, Pete Fetzer, Sr. wrote this assessment in their guest book. "*Too bad this bunch couldn't find anything to do here. Nothing but swimming, acqua-planeing (sic), sailing, motor boating, canoeing, rowing, putt-putt, piano, bridge, movies, carbonated belly wash, ping pong, tennis, eating, sleeping (occasionally)—such a bore.*" Someone added, "*Don't forget the free movies in Glen Arbor.*"

There was an inside understanding that potential spouses needed to pass the "Glen Lake test" before they were brought into the family fold. This simply meant that when they visited, they needed to love the area's beauty and fit into a relaxed life shared with nature. The Addoms family test included being able to navigate the traps and culvert of the Crystal River together in a canoe. Chick Lanphier brought his Southern bride north for her first visit on their honeymoon. He loved it here and thought it romantic to spend a few days on the dunes. The wind started to blow and sand got everywhere in the tent. Even Chick's fried eggs had sand in them. The campout only lasted 24 hours before they returned in one of the old dune buggies. But she passed the "Glen Lake test."

Family pride and tradition also surrounded summer's activities. It was heard more than once than "no other family could have ever had as much fun as theirs." Fun, games and traditions were invented. The Fetzer family began an annual clam race in 1948. Over the years additional heats were added, adding more names on the yearly trophy boards carved in wood that hang in the cottage. One fact is undisputed: the clams have slowed down and don't move as far during this two-day race as they used to.

In the late 1940s this unidentified guest book tribute was written in a child's handwriting.

"*Everybody in this book may read this because I have something important but very nice to say about the lake and the Fetzer family. I've been up here every since I was born practicaly (sic). I have seen many new and well-earned changes come over the cabins, but the people of the Fetzer family will never change. Margaret Fetzer I'm sure worked hard and long to make this place what it is today. Everyone can come up here for a real whopper of a vacation. When I stop to think every Fetzer belonging to this clan has a great number of things to be thankful for. In future years I hope the Fetzer generation will still be helping to make our "family" even more proud of our "Glen Lake"!*"

And so summer passed with carefree sunny days giving way to nights filled with laughter and socializing as the sun set over the Sleeping Bear. Daytime sounds of motorboats, competitive games and picnics hushed at twilight. Cottagers slept well lulled by the lapping water and soothing breezes. Indeed, these were the idyllic times, likened to paradise, that linger in the memories of all who summered on Glen Lake's shores.

Barbara and Nate Whiteside sailing their modified dinghy.
(*Whiteside Family Collection*)

The Cottages

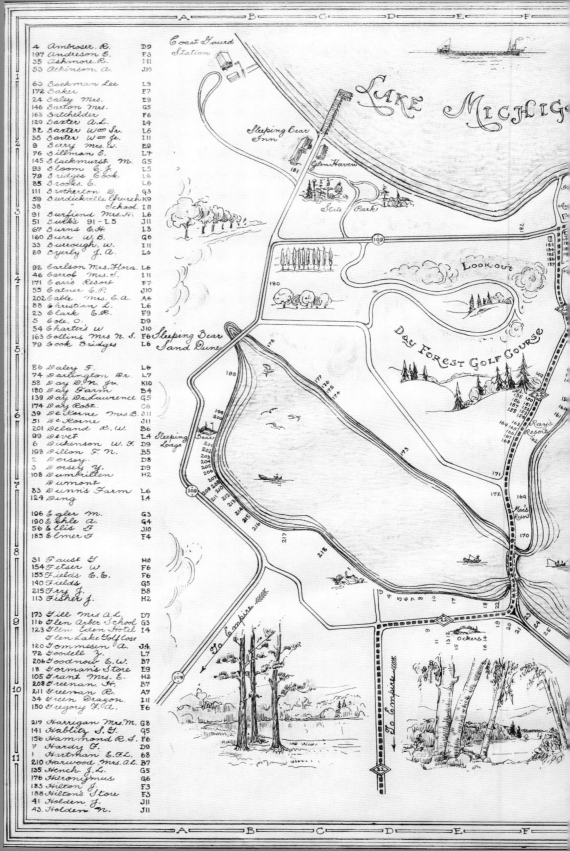

Glen Lake Map ©Arthur Gommesen, circa 1939

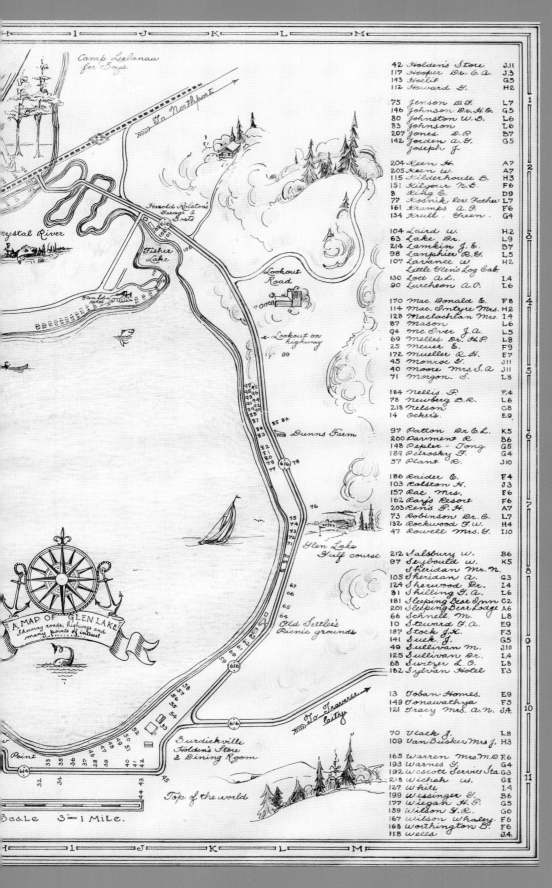

A MAP OF GLEN LAKE
Showing roads, highways and many points of interest

Scale 3" = 1 Mile.

Camp Leelanau for Boys

To Northport

Crystal River

Harold Rolston's Garage & Boats

Fisher Lake

Lookout Road

Lookout on highway

Dunns Farm

Glen Lake Golf course

Old Settler's Picnic grounds

To Traverse City

Burdickville
Holden's Store & Dining Room

Top of the world

#	Name	Loc
42	Holden's Store	J.11
117	Hooper Dr. C.A.	J.3
143	Hoelit	G.5
112	Howard	H.2
75	Jenson D.F.	L.7
146	Johnson Dr. H.C.	G.5
80	Johnston W.B.	L.6
83	Johnson	L.6
207	Jones D.P.	B.7
142	Jorden A.G.	G.5
	Joseph J.	
204	Keen H.	A.7
205	Keen W.	A.7
115	Kilderhouse B.	H.3
151	Kilgour C.	
8	King E.	D.9
77	Kosnik Rev. Fathr	L.7
161	Kramps A.F.	F.6
134	Krull . Green	G.4
104	Laird W.	H.2
63	Lake Dr.	L.9
214	Lamkin J.E.	B.7
98	Lanphier R.C.	L.5
107	Larance W	H.2
	Little Glen's Log Cab.	
130	Lott A.L.	L.4
90	Lurcheon A.O.	L.6
170	Mac Donald E.	F.8
114	Mac Intyre Mrs.	H.2
128	Maclachlan Mrs.	I.4
87	Mason	L.6
94	Mc Iver J.A.	L.5
69	Melles Dr. H.P.	L.8
25	Meuer E.	F.9
172	Mueller R.H.	E.7
45	Monroe J.	J.11
40	Moore Mrs. S.A.	J.11
71	Morgon S.	L.8
184	Nellis P.	F.4
78	Newberg B.R.	L.6
218	Nelson	C.8
14	Ockers	E.9
97	Patton Dr. C.L.	K.5
200	Parment R.	B.6
148	Pepler - Jong	G.5
189	Petrosky F.	G.4
57	Plant R.	J.10
186	Raider E.	F.4
103	Rolston H.	J.3
157	Rae Mrs.	F.6
162	Ray's Resort	F.6
203	Ren's P.H.	A.7
73	Robinson Dr. G.	L.7
132	Rockwood F.W.	H.4
47	Rowell Mrs. G.	I.10
212	Salsbury W.	B.6
97	Seybould W.	K.5
	Sheridan Mr. N.	
105	Sheridan A.	G.3
124	Sherwood Dr.	I.4
81	Shilling J.A.	L.6
181	Sleeping Bear Inn	C.2
201	Sleeping Bear Lodge	A.6
66	Schnell M.	L.8
10	Steward J.A.	E.9
187	Stock J.K.	F.3
141	Suek J.	G.5
49	Sullivan M.	J.10
125	Sullivan Dr.	I.4
68	Switzer L.O.	L.8
182	Sylvan Hotel	F.3
13	Toban Homes	E.9
149	Tonawathya	F.5
121	Tracy Mrs. A.N.	J.4
70	Vlack J.	L.8
109	Van Busker Mrs J.	H.3
165	Warren Mrs. M.D.	F.6
193	Warnes G.	G.4
192	Wescott Service Sta.	G.3
218	Wichah W.	G.8
127	White	I.4
199	Wessinger G.	B.6
177	Wiegan H.P.	G.5
159	Wilson G.R.	G.6
167	Wilson Whaley	F.6
168	Worthington B.	F.6
118	Wells	J.4

THE COTTAGES

DeWitt Cottage, 1959

Crosby Cottage

WALKER HOUSE

Pinetum   *(Kroeber-Fornowski Family Collection)*

Dr. William H. and Elizabeth A. Walker followed their friend John E. Fisher to Glen Arbor from Fond du Lac, Wisconsin. Dr. Walker served as an army surgeon. In 1858 they purchased this property and about seven other parcels on a land grant from the U.S. Government. Fisher owned east of Lake Street and Walker west of Lake Street where he built an in-town house. Walker named this Glen Lake residence, *Glenwood Park*. It was likely built around the time he established Michigan's second largest cranberry operation in about 1870.

The cranberry bog was located in the swamp on the east side of M-22 between Glen Arbor and Glen Lake. After removing the cedar and white pine trees, ditches were dug and water pumped from Glen Lake to keep the plants from freezing in the winter. The ditches were drained in the spring and the berries individually picked during September by about one hundred Native Americans from Peshawbestown, north of Suttons Bay. The workers stayed in a two-story barrack to the south of the marsh. Hun-

dreds of barrels, which were made locally, were used to ship the cranberry harvest to Chicago and Detroit.

In 1888 Dr. Walker left the property to his son William, Jr. and his wife Minnie along with the apple orchard they had helped establish on the property between the bog and the house. The Walkers lived in the house until 1917 when they sold to John C. and Myrtle E. Suek who later sold off much of the property. After living there thirty years, Myrtle sold the house after WWII and it then changed hands a few times. In 1947, the Gregorys and Evelyn Kroeber purchased it and it became known as *Pinetum*.

Robert W. and June (Essley) Nissen from Hinsdale, Illinois, purchased the house in 1958. They had twin daughters, Deborah and Judy. The house contained a wood-burning stove built in Kalamazoo that dated from the early 1920s. They have not made any changes except for adding a downstairs bathroom. The water pump still stands in the front yard.

Circa 1870s

William and Elizabeth Walker House

House: Two-story wood farm-style house clad in narrow lap-siding

Interior: Stucco plastered walls with thick rope moldings, living room with fieldstone chimney which has been painted, dining room, kitchen, office, and four bedrooms on second floor

Outbuildings: Garage/workshop across the road, boathouse with changing rooms at base of bluff

Frontage: 135 feet

Map Location: G5, #141

MILLER • BROTHERTON • DeVette House

MID-1870S

SILAS AND SARAH MILLER •
DAN AND ELLEN BROTHERTON •
FRANK AND JESSIE DeVETTE HOUSE

COTTAGE: Two-story, seven-room wood farmhouse with narrow lap-siding and wide decorative barge board (not original)

INTERIOR: Living room, dining room, kitchen, front porch, three bedrooms

ADDITION: Large front porch likely in 1925

OUTBUILDING: Garage and workshop

MAP LOCATION: L4, #99

This farmhouse, located near the base of Miller Hill, is on property homesteaded in 1862 by the Reverend Daniel and Ann (Hart) Miller. Sons Wells and Marshall homesteaded adjacent 160-acre plots. They established apple, cherry and pear orchards and shipped to the Chicago market from Glen Haven. Rev. Miller was an itinerate minister who rode a horse to hold services in schools and home and sometimes led three services on a Sunday. He donated land for the Miller Hill School.

Daniel's younger son Silas married Sarah Tucker, daughter of Bishop Tucker, and took ownership of 23 acres in 1872. It was likely that Silas built this house about that time. His widow sold the property to Dan and Ellen Brotherton in 1888. In 1913 the Brothertons leased the apple trees to the Glencrest Orchard Company for an annual fee of fifty cents per tree. Frank and Jessie DeVette purchased the farm in 1925 for $4000. Frank was a carpenter and fishing guide. In recent years the house has served as a summer vacation residence.

The farmhouse sits on the east side of Dunn's Farm Road overlooking the lake. The kitchen has a Detroit-made Jewell cook stove and the dining room cabinetry is original. Decorative Victorian barge trim was added later. Two huge trees that flanked the front steps were recently cut down as they were uprooting the large glassed front porch.

EVELYN'S COTTAGE *(Brown Cottage)*

John August and Hilda (Kant) Johnson worked for Anna and Frank A. Gregory during the time the Gregorys lived on the south side of Chicago. They also came with the Gregorys to Glen Lake and worked at the Gregory's Tonawathya Resort. August Johnson, born in Germany, was the butler and maintenance man. Hilda, whose family was from Sweden, worked as housekeeper for the resort. In the early years they lived in this cottage and a well-stocked tool dresser remains on the side porch. Their daughter Evelyn was older than her brother Herb who was born in this cottage in 1906. Herb never married and worked for the Chicago postal service.

This cottage originally had birch bark porch railings. It stood just south of the Inn and was named *Brown Cottage*. It was built and maintained by Tonawathya. It was likely given to Evelyn J. and John K. Kroeber in September 1944 at which time the cottage became known as Evelyn's Cottage. The Gregorys had no children and cared for Evelyn as if she were their own child. They sent her to the School of Domestic Arts and Sciences at the University of Chicago where she studied to become a teacher. John and Evelyn met when he was a Michigan State student living at Glen Lake for a summer forestry camp in 1928 or 1929. He was a determined young man who knew what he wanted to do

with his life. He accepted a challenge to swim across the lake to take Evelyn as his date to a social held at Tonawathya. They were married in April 1930. The Kroebers lived in East Lansing where he worked his entire career with Michigan Department of Forestry. He traveled extensively and became in charge of the eastern half of Michigan. They had no children.

The unwinterized cottage had a living/dining room, kitchen, front porch, and two bedrooms. It retains the original wallpaper, a library table, highboy, and an Indian print above the fireplace, referred to as *Tonawathya. Wren Cottage*, an original one-bedroom Tonawathya rental cottage without kitchen facilities, sits to the northwest of this cottage and is used as a guest house.

The cottage was inherited by John Kroeber's nephew, Ronald Fornowski, who sold it to Almon and Norma Durkee in 1981. The Durkees had purchased a cottage near the Narrows on Glen Lake a few years before they purchased this cottage. They have seven children, Dee, David, Deb, Doug, Don, Darren and Darrell.

EARLY 1900s

JOHN AND EVELYN KROEBER COTTAGE
(Brown Cottage)

EVELYN'S COTTAGE: Wood frame construction clad with lap-siding, brick fireplace, living/dining room, kitchen, front porch, two bedrooms

1988 ADDITION: Bedroom built from walls salvaged from the Kilgour Cottage to the south when it was torn down by the Ronald and Charlotte Fornowski when they built their new home

WREN COTTAGE: Original two-room Tonawathya cottage,

FOOTAGE: 100 feet

MAP LOCATION: F6, not numbered

Evelyn Kroeber visiting with Frank and Anna Gregory on their 80th birthdays in 1946
(Fornowski Family Collection)

WORTHINGTON COTTAGE *(Birchworth)*

Gerrit and Sue (Ingman) Worthington came to Gregory's via boat to Glen Haven soon after the Gregorys began their resort, Tonawathya, on the west shore of Glen Lake. The Worthingtons were from Oak Park, Illinois, where he worked at an insurance company. It is likely they had known the Gregorys before their first visit. Once here they commenced to fall in love with Glen Lake and purchased a southern corner of the Gregory's property to build a cottage for their family of three children, Virginia (Bogle), LaGrange and Robert I. It cost $500 to build the cottage in 1907.

One evening Mrs. Worthington was walking home on the cow path that ran behind the cottages from Gregory's to her cottage when she heard footsteps behind her. As she walked more rapidly, the footsteps kept pace with her. When she reached the porch light and turned around, she found that it was a calf from Gregory's farm that had followed her home. One of the two cow pastures was behind their cottage.

During the summers of 1910-1914, son Robert worked for Mrs. Gregory. He and another young man working in the meadow cut out a piece of sod and hid a checkerboard beneath it, so that they could play checkers while they were supposed to be working. Mrs. Gregory, who closely supervised her large staff, never found them out.

After Robert married, he bought the white wicker porch furniture to celebrate his son Robert W.'s birth in 1930. His wife planned the Tonawathya Inn's meals and kept the books from 1939-1944. When son Robert turned twelve he had a job weeding the garden for Mrs. Gregory. One day he decided he could do this kneeling down or better yet lying down and continuing to weed with one arm. Out of the corner of his eye, he saw this white gown approaching, watching, never saying a word, just observing. He was always frightened by Mrs. Gregory and dreaded having to pass her in the hallway, yet he remembers these as glorious years. "The apogee of life is sitting on the dock

in the sunshine at Glen Lake and everything else declines from there; other life experiences are not important."

A boathouse was built in 1914 to house the large white wooden inboard motorboat named *Birch Bark*. The Worthingtons enjoyed dressing up and pulling up to Mrs. Gregory's dock for Sunday dinner. A dress code was strictly enforced and guests could not be seated until Mrs. Gregory was seated. The Worthington's other son LaGrange raced and once won the Motor Boat Race, a part of an annual regatta held at Gregory's. The boat was sold during the Depression.

In 1939 the Worthingtons rotated the boathouse, moved it across M-22, added a porch and turned it into a guest cottage in front of the original cottage. It continues to be used when the weather is too cold to stay in the un-heated main cottage. The cottage remains in the family with most of the original furniture and has been the center of important family events.

Worthington's wood boat *Birch Bark*, 1920s *(Worthington Family Collection)*

Worthington Cottage   *(Whiteside Family Collection)*

1907

Gerrit and Sue Worthington Cottage
(Birchworth)

Cottage: Wood frame construction clad with painted lap-siding

Interior: Natural horizontally laid beaded board interior walls and ceiling and wood floors; living room with brick fireplace (added several years later); three bedrooms (two with open stud construction); screened front porch with wide wood flooring, originally was open with birch bark railings; original separate kitchen

1922 Addition: Kitchen attached to the cottage when they hired a local cook; porch extended to wrap around to the kitchen and hold dining table

Outbuildings: Boathouse turned into a two-room cottage after it was moved across M-22; tall skinny icehouse dismantled in exchange for the 100 pounds of honey it contained

Frontage: 300 feet

Map Location: F6, #168

BRAY COTTAGE

Bray cottage with family in 1918   *(Dickinson Family Collection)*

Joseph Thomas and Elizabeth (Danson) Bray from Chicago learned about Glen Lake when the principal of the school where their daughter Gladys taught told them about Cedar Springs Resort on the north shore of Little Glen. They first visited in 1912 with their children Ruth (Dickinson), Gladys (Cole), Harry and James. Bray was a cabinet maker and finish carpenter who had learned his trade in England. He built many Chicago public building staircases. He also built two for the Mormon Tabernacle that were shipped to Salt Lake City with numbered pieces and instructions.

In 1914 while constructing their two-story cottage on the south shore of Little Glen, they stayed a month at nearby King's Kenwood and the rest of the summer at Gregory's Tonawathya. The finishing wood, including the living room cedar paneling and French doors, was shipped to Glen Haven from Wilce Lumber in Chicago, the same

company that had a lumber operation in Empire. The cottage was placed on log piers that were later replaced with a foundation and Michigan cellar. Insulation was newspaper in the walls. A year later the fireplace and front porch were added. The original blueprint called the bedrooms "chambers". Bray, a perfectionist and artist, did much of the work himself and also built the fireplace for Dickinson's cottage next door.

Ruth Bray married William Frederick Dickinson in 1907. They had met in Chicago when she was an art student at the Art Institute of Chicago. The Dickinsons lived in Oak Park, Illinois, until they moved to Hinsdale in 1919. Dickinson was a prominent Chicago attorney and was vice-president of the Rock Island Railroad. They spent summers at Glen Lake and built a cottage just to the east of her parents in 1923. They had two sons, Frederick William born in 1907 and Robert James who was two years

Living room in 1918 *(Dickinson Family Collection)*

younger. Ruth continued to add additions to the cottage. It is currently for sale and has been changed significantly.

Gladys Bray married Charles Cole with whom she owned a printing company in Chicago. They had two children, Charles, Jr. and Elizabeth. Elizabeth inherited this cottage from her parents but later sold it. It has had several owners since, including Dr. Gerald Behan whose family (Clark) had originally owned an old cottage on the southwest corner of Glen Lake.

Joseph and Kathleen Wiesen purchased this cottage sometime in the in the early 1970s from Fred and Dorothy Glock when they moved their family of eight children to Glen Lake. At one time the Wiesens owned all of the taverns and two motels in Empire and Glen Arbor. The cottage integrity has been retained and its charm enhanced with decorating and kitchen updates.

1914

Joseph and Elizabeth Bray Cottage

Cottage: Two-story wood frame construction covered with lap-siding

Interior: Living room, kitchen, six bedrooms

Outbuildings: Garage built in 1917, icehouse that also serviced neighbors in 1919, and guesthouse moved from Empire's Salisbury Cottages

Frontage: 175 feet

Map Location: D9, #5

FRALICK • LEHMANN COTTAGE

This two-story bungalow cottage was built in 1917 by one of Leelanau County's best-known and beloved residents, Dr. George W. Fralick. In 1893, after graduating from the Michigan College of Medicine and Surgery in Detroit and marrying Minerva E. Ernest, Dr. Fralick established his office and home in Maple City. He made house calls by horse and buggy and later in the county's first automobile. His buggy is displayed in the Empire Historical Museum. He, his wife and only child Orpha spent summers at their Glen Lake cottage. It is located in a subdivision known as Sewama Heights which was platted about 1916 by Maple City and Cedar businessmen for their families and for investment. A tenting camp predated the building of cottages on this property and 12' x 12' platforms have been found. In the late 1800s, it was the site of a lumber camp belonging to Nessen's Glen Arbor Lumber Company.

Following the death of both parents in 1924, Orpha, a schoolteacher in Traverse City, Michigan, married Howard E. Burfiend, grandson of the founder of nearby Port Oneida. They built a family home on the Burfiend farm in Port Oneida. She kept and used the family cottage and rented out at least one other cottage that they also owned.

In 1936 Orpha sold the family cottage to Charles Frederick and Jessie Ellen (McKenzie) Lehmann of Delphos, Ohio, owners of Lehmann Furniture. With their children, Margaret (Krueger), Morris and Dorothy (Husted), they had been renting in the area since 1930s, having heard about the clean air. The family made the cottage their own by naming it *Glen Ellen*. German artisans in north central Ohio handcrafted the cottage furniture. The Lehmanns also purchased adjacent cottages, once part of the lumber camp, until they had seven rental cottages plus

1917

GEORGE W. AND MINERVA FRALICK • CHARLES AND JESSIE LEHMANN COTTAGE

COTTAGE: Two-story bungalow wood frame cottage with dormers, clad in narrow double lap-siding, originally painted white with green trim, large fieldstone chimney and porch pillar bases, eight-light casement windows

INTERIOR: Pine beaded board walls, living room, kitchen, four second-floor bedrooms with open roof rafters

OUTBUILDINGS: Garage with attached outhouse; small gatehouse by the road (torn down); boathouse (later a guest cottage at the base of the bluff); barn across the road built for Lehmann's riding horses (torn down)

LANDSCAPE FEATURE: Cement sidewalk across the front of the two original properties

FRONTAGE: 133 feet in Sewama Heights subdivision

MAP LOCATION: L6, #91

Glen Ellen, known as Glen Ayr Resort. Upon the Lehmanns' deaths, the children divided the property.

Margaret and her husband, Fritz Krueger, who were musicians in the Philadelphia area, inherited *Glen Ellen*. Margaret was a concert pianist and organist and Fritz was a tenor soloist with the Philadelphia Opera Company. They often had friends over to the cottage for musical evenings. The cottage retains two pianos and a pump organ.

The Krueger's children, Karen and John, inherited the cottage. Karen's sentiment about retaining the essence of the old cottage intact was so strong that a 2002 addition was designed to attach at the back corner of the kitchen so that the original cottage remained unchanged and un-winterized. The new addition duplicated the rare narrow double lap-siding with mitered corners and eight-light casement windows that open inward. During the renovation, the cottage was found to be without a foundation but rested on a stump and a rock at each of the four corners. A new foundation was poured in four sections and nine yards of cement went under the chimney. The chimney had pulled away from the cottage in the 1960s and the space filled with smaller rocks.

DILLON COTTAGE *(Crocodillonbear)*

(Dillon Family Collection)

Frank Dillon, a commercial artist and instructor at the Art Institute of Chicago, first came by ship to Glen Haven in 1904 as a teenager. He was accompanied by his high school photographer friend, Walker Jamar, who had been here before. They tented at Kenwood Resort on the south side of Little Glen. Jamar took pictures of them hiking, picnicking and boating dressed in the somewhat formal attire of the day.

Alice Goss had been one of Frank's art students. They married in 1911 and honeymooned at Kenwood. She illustrated for a card company and children's magazine. In Winnetka, Illinois, they raised a family of four children, Ralph, Barrie (Jack Riday), Ananda (Ben Bricker) and Ariel (Dean Schrader). They have many artist-descendants over four generations.

In 1918 the Dillons purchased property on the west side of Little Glen across from what is now the Dune Climb. They had a two-bedroom prefabricated kit home

shipped to Glen Haven along with a set of Indiana Hickory Log Furniture. A fieldstone chimney was built from rocks gathered at the narrows and brought by many rowboat trips to the property. The two-bedroom cottage originally had an open porch facing the lake. The kitchen in the back had a hand-pump and an icebox filled with ice cut from Glen Lake the preceding winter. The water was piped into the cottage to operate the flush toilet from the water tank on top of the garage. The kitchen door frame has all the children's heights marked on it.

The Dillons brought their parents and grandparents to Glen Lake for vacations. Frank's sister Gladys and her husband Bruce Young built a cottage next door. Her nickname was "Babe", and the Dillons named their wooden launch *Babe*. They owned the launch before they had a cottage and kept it at Kenwood Resort. The children had a sandbox next to the cottage. They sat upon and "rode" logs that washed ashore from the huge log rafts being towed to the

Babe, Dillon's wood launch, at Kenwood Resort boathouse

(Dillon Family Collection)

Grandfather and Barrie playing in the sand box

(Dillon Family Collection)

Four year old Barrie "riding" the log

(Dillon Family Collection)

Kitchen   (*Dillon Family Collection*)

D.H. Day sawmill on the millpond located on the northwest corner of Little Glen Lake. Barrie had a horse and rode alone as a teenager around the lake and through the dunes. They named their cottage *Crocodillonbear* referring to their family name for Alligator Hill and their location between it and the Sleeping Bear Dune. It felt to them as if the Bear in their backyard was their own and they climbed it daily.

When Frank retired to Glen Lake, he began teaching art at the Leelanau School in Glen Arbor. Over the years the cottage has been filled with heirlooms and works of art by family and friends. The spirit of the original cottage, now owned by the Brickers, has been maintained through the years. The garage and remodeled guest cottage are now owned by the Ridays of Seattle, Washington. The Ridays and Brickers went to high school together in Winnetka, Illinois. Ananda and Ben Bricker married in 1942, honeymooning in the cottage in winter without a car. They walked a long day from/to Frankfort for the ferry that came across Lake Michigan. They grocery shopped in Glen Arbor pulling a toboggan. When the Brickers moved here permanently in 1983, Ananda created her ceramic Forest Flowers business. Ananda and Ben were founders of Glen Lake Artists Gallery and co-founders of the Glen Arbor Art Association.

1918

FRANK H. AND ALICE DILLON COTTAGE (*Crocodillonbear*)

COTTAGE: One-story precut kit frame cottage, likely Sears and Roebuck, with flat cedar shingle and shutters

INTERIOR: Living room with stone chimney, kitchen, two bedrooms

1950S ADDITION: Art studio when Dillon moved permanently to Glen Lake, screened porch became part of the living room

MID-1980S ADDITION: Garage, two upstairs guest rooms, studio designed by architect Don Wilson, and an attic loft bedroom

OUTBUILDINGS: Garage and guest house (now on property owned by Ridays) had a horse stall and 4 x 4 posts which extended through the roof to support the water tank, fed by a "one lunger" engine in the icehouse; icehouse moved to edge of the lake and used for overflow guests

FRONTAGE: 200 feet (now 135 after division of property)

MAP LOCATION: B5, #198

WARREN • SENTER COTTAGE

This one-story cottage was thought to be built for A.H. and Mary Dell Warren and their two children of Hinsdale, Illinois, by the Gregorys who owned the adjacent Tonawathya Inn. Originally a wide stone and cement central staircase led into the living area but was later enclosed and became a twin bedroom. After Mrs. Warren was widowed, she continued to spend her summers here and was a well-liked neighbor. John Dorsey remembers delivering milk to her.

The cottage was sold to William and Geraldine Mirgeler who rented it for a short time and enclosed part of the back porch to make an eat-in kitchen. In 1955 they sold it to Detroit friends, Richard and Hortense Senter and their four children, Richard, Jr. (Mary), Stephen (Debbie), Robin (Peter McKenna) and Laurel (David Jeris). Senter, an attorney, served in the FBI and did legal law enforcement training for police throughout Michigan. The Senters had been renting at Niles Edgewater Resort near the narrows since 1948 after previously vacationing in Bay View, Petoskey, Michigan. The children observed their mother transform as she "drank in the beauty of Glen Lake."

Hortense referred to their treasured Glen Lake times as "wool gathering" and although undefined, the children knew this meant no TV or telephone and lots of make-believe games, reading and solitude. She read classics to her children and did not have to stop at the end of the chapter as there was no need to get up early for school. A believer in family outings, Hortense would take the children on all-day painting excursions in addition to swimming, boating and climbing the Dunes. They would practice climbing the sawdust hill at the Stocking's sawmill before climbing the Dunes. Her painting of Fish Town hangs over the fireplace. When they had guests, the parents chose to sleep in the remodeled lumber camp cookhouse they had moved from their property on Wheeler road. The Senter children and their spouses continue to own this virtually unchanged cottage with some of the original furniture and books.

1918
A.H. AND MARY WARREN • RICHARD AND HORTENSE SENTER COTTAGE

COTTAGE: One-story wood frame cottage clad with painted wood shingles

INTERIOR: Living room with fieldstone fireplace, beaded board interior walls and ceiling (later painted white), Douglas-fir floors, two bedrooms, back porch

OUTBUILDINGS: Shingled garage with attached outhouse, one bedroom guest house is former lumber camp cookhouse moved in about 1980

FRONTAGE: 100 feet

MAP LOCATION: F6, #165

Dunbar • Batchelder • Williams Cottage

Circa 1920

Dunbar • Batchelder • Williams Cottage

Cottage: One-story wood frame clad in painted narrow lap-siding

Interior: Living/dining room with brick fireplace, beaded board ceiling and walls, kitchen, screened porch the length of the cottage, two bedrooms, Celotex hallway

Addition: Two bedrooms prior to Williams' ownership

Outbuildings: Carriage house turned into heated guest house in early 1970s, outhouse

Frontage: 170 feet

Map Location: F6, #163

William M. and Georgia Dunbar likely built this cottage after purchasing the property in 1920. In 1926, George H. and Francis T. Batchelder purchased it from Dunbars. The Batchelder's artistic daughter Helen made a painting of the back of the cottage as seen from Tonawathya's cow pasture. The painting still hangs on the cottage wall. Helen inherited the cottage and sold it in 1945 to Robert G. and Helene Williams from LaGrange, Illinois, where he was president of LaGrange National Bank. With their four daughters, twins Joan and Betty, Anne and Sara, they spent many wonderful years on Glen Lake.

After Williams retired to Arkansas in about 1970, he sold the cottage on land contract to Dr. Bruce Greenfield, former son-in-law of the Addoms who lived in the cottage to the south. Everett and Katherine (Beatty) Addoms,

were from Beloit, Wisconsin, where he headed a large machinery stamping business. They had four children, Sally, Sam, and twins, Elizabeth and Mary. Their cottage had originally been built by Sam and Elizabeth Beatty of Hinsdale, Illinois, where he was an industrialist. When the Beattys purchased a large tract of land on Sandy Cove on the north shore of Glen Lake, they sold the cottage to two teachers, Miss Wilson and Miss Whaley. Beatty's daughter, Kit, purchased the cottage from them. After Kit sold it in the early 1990s, the cottage was torn down.

The property originally included the road and southern cow pasture that ran behind the cottages. The pasture was sold to the Sleeping Bear National Lakeshore when the government was acquiring property for the park. The cottage remains virtually unchanged.

HENCH • SYMONDS COTTAGE

Jay Lyman and Rachel (Cable) Hench began coming to Glen Lake in 1921. They were searching for a spot where their eldest daughter Katherine could receive swimming therapy to strengthen her polio-weakened legs. For several years they stayed at Gregory's Tonawathya Resort with their daughters, Katherine (Whitney), Helen (Jones) and Fayette (Johnson). The family stayed for the summer and Mr. Hench, a Chicago businessman, commuted every weekend by boat.

By 1928 they had purchased one of the existing cottages from the Gregorys on the hill side of M-22. The Henches renovated the one-story cottage from plans drawn up in Hinsdale, Illinois, where they lived. As the family continued to take their meals at the resort, no kitchen facilities were included.

In 1944 the Henches had the opportunity to purchase a larger cottage with more lake frontage on Sunset Drive. Helen (Spiece) Collings had built the cottage after her marriage to Fletcher Hemstead Field. After her death, Field sold *Dreamwood* to the Henches. When Dr. Lawrence Day offered them his log cottage and office by the side of the road, to the east of them, the Henches also purchased it.

It is interesting to note that some thirty years later, two Hench daughters, Katherine and Helen, purchased Old

Orchard Resort, formerly known as Tonawathya, and ran it until a consultant recommended they raze the Inn.

Nathaniel Millberry and Johnetta (Marshall) Symonds and their children Nathaniel Marshall and Eleanor Margaret (Deng) were friends of the Henches and purchased this photographed cottage in 1946. They had been renting the *Hill Cottage* at Tonawathya for several years. After the purchase, despite the challenge of acquiring appliances at end of World War II, their first priority was to add a kitchen by enclosing part of the open side porch. Symonds was a Chicago banker and Hinsdale Village President from 1965 until he died in 1968.

Roswell D. and Vivian Jennings purchased the cottage from the estate and built a new home in the location of the guest cottage. They also retained the integrity of this cottage during a 1980s restoration. It has many of the original furnishings.

EARLY 1920S
JAY AND RACHEL HENCH • NATHANIEL AND JOHNETTA SYMONDS COTTAGE

COTTAGE: One-story wood frame cottage clad with stained narrow lap-siding

1928 RENOVATION: Of original Tonawathya Cottage; living room, two sleeping porches, two dressing rooms, front and side porches with birch bark railings.

1946 RENOVATION: Part of the side porch made into a kitchen

OUTBUILDINGS: One-bedroom guest cottage (removed in the 1980s), sand floor boathouse (now a garage)

FRONTAGE: 200 feet

MAP LOCATION: G5, #135

Kay Hench, Sunny Brooks and Helen Hench
(Doepke Family Collection)

JONES COTTAGE *(Dunworkin)*

James Herbert Jones, a dentist by profession but an adventurer at heart, loved to explore, camp, and deer hunt. He first came to the area when he and his cousin became the first campers in the D.H. Day State Park. In 1922, Herb and his wife Lulu purchased a 100 foot lot on the west shore of Little Glen Lake for $500. He designed and built a cottage in 1923 with lumber picked up from the dock at Glen Haven by a team of horses and wagon. They camped on the property while building the cottage and garage. At that time the road (M-109) ran alongside the lake prior to its being moved to its present location behind the cottage.

Considering that the 232-mile drive from their home in Parma, Michigan, to Glen Lake took a day and a half, the family would spend lengthy vacations at their cottage. They fished from a rowboat near Alligator Hill, motored on the Glen Lakes in the large cabin cruiser Jones built and enjoyed a smaller motor boat on Little Glen accessed by a two-plank dock.

When Dr. Jones retired, he spent more time at the cottage which he named *Dunworkin*, and his hand-carved sign still hangs above the porch door. He remodeled the

Front yard camping, during construction 1923 *(Jones Family Collection)*

A rocking break from cottage construction *(Jones Family Collection)*

Jack Jones *gonefishin'*, 1925   *(Jones Family Collection)*

Cabin crusier built by F. Herbert Jones   *(Jones Family Collection)*

cottage in 1949, adding a bedroom and bathroom which eliminated the necessity of an outhouse. Next to the garage and beside the well pump, he built a washstand and fireplace which features adjustable grates plus a grate in the chimney for smoking fish. Both are still in use. Dr. Jones and their youngest son Jack, also a dentist, built some of the cottage furniture, using tools from the well organized and hand-labeled workshop in the garage. Rocking chairs, in the family for over fifty years, are lined up on the front porch. A favorite activity of the elder Joneses was "rocking to Traverse City" while watching the youngsters play on the beach.

Jack and his wife Charlotte vacationed only at Glen Lake; it's just what the family did, a tradition that ensured strong memories and close family ties. The cottage remains in the family and is now owned by their youngest son Gary and his wife Barbara. They reside in Virginia but continue to vacation at the Jones Cottage, an 805-mile trip. They have two children, Gary II and Julie, and are proud to have their grandchildren as fifth generation cottage lovers.

1923

J. HERBERT AND LULU JONES COTTAGE *(Dunworkin)*

BUILDER: J. Herbert Jones and C. A. Cable

COTTAGE: One-story, wood frame cottage with narrow Dutch-lap siding painted white with green trim, open stud construction with tapered round and cut fieldstone chimney

INTERIOR: Living room, two bedrooms, kitchen and front porch

1949 ADDITION AND REMODELING: Cut fieldstone fireplace front, knotty-pine tongue-and-groove paneling with wide Dutch-lap siding on bedroom addition; Charlie Fast assisted with the building

OUTBUILDINGS: Two-car garage and workshop, two-hole wooden outhouse, second one-car garage was acquired when more property was purchased to the south

FRONTAGE: 100 feet, additional 50 later

MAP LOCATION: B7, #207

Hartmann Cottage

Ernest F.L. Hartmann was of English descent and a direct descendant of Sir John Hawkins, cousin to Sir Frances Drake. In Canada he served in the Royal Canadian Mounted Police. After he moved to Chicago, Illinois, he worked for McGraw-Hill. He had been coming to Glen Lake since the early 1900s by ship and camped out near Inspiration Point on Burdickville Hill with his sister Amy's family from Muskegon. Amy was married to Hugo Kranitz.

In 1923 he had an Aladdin Redi-Cut summer cottage shipped from Bay City, Michigan, by train to Cedar. It is a 20' x 30' Luna model and has #23562 stamped on the attic rafter. Hartmann constructed the cottage on the south shore of Little Glen on land he purchased from his neighbor George Dorsey who became a good friend. They would visit on Dorsey's porch. John Dorsey remembers books that Hartmann brought him and later became the cottage caretaker.

Ernest's wife's name was Erma and it is thought she died before the cottage was constructed. Hartmann drove here in a Pierce Arrow. Later his son, Chester, drove him in his black Studebaker. Chester was in real estate; his sister Gladys was a church organist and singer. Both lived with their father in Chicago and at Glen Lake for the summer months as neither married. Chester enjoyed collecting sand and rocks from the lake and placed them along the cottage shore. Erma's sister, Irene Lewis, often visited from her home in Pentwater, Michigan, and would cook for the family. For many years, the Kanitz family continued the summer cottage vacation tradition even after the Hartmanns were no longer able to use the cottage.

Norbert and Joanne Sprouse purchased this cottage in 1979. It was situated on a lot in front of their cottage and partially blocked their view of Glen Lake. They used it first as a guest cottage and later as a rental. The cottage was later taken off its cedar log piers and moved east onto a new foundation and sold to John and Shirley Peters in 1992. The Peters decided to purchase when they walked in and spotted the hand-colored Wabash River photograph on the wall. John's father had grown up on the river and had just gifted them a down payment for a cottage.

1923

ERNEST HARTMANN COTTAGE

COTTAGE: One-story pine frame Aladdin Redi-cut cottage with open studs and covered with cedar wide Dutch-lap tongue-and-groove siding and exposed rafter ends

INTERIOR: Living room, kitchen, three small bedrooms and screen enclosed porch on the lake side; fieldstone fireplace, kitchen and bathroom added after original construction

1979 RENOVATION: One bedroom wall removed to make a larger bedroom

1992 RENOVATION: Changed back porch addition roof line and re-exposed rafter ends of original structure in kitchen and bathroom

OUTBUILDINGS: Shed, pump house, sun-heated water tank on raised posts with shower underneath (no longer standing)

SHED/GARAGE: Built in 1968 by Hugo Kanitz, nephew of Mr. Hartmann from Muskegon, when he moved a double-wide mobile home onto the property

FRONTAGE: 150 feet

MAP LOCATION: C8, #1

ROBINSON COTTAGE

Camp Davis, Burdickville, Michigan, 1908
(*Vintage Views Archives*)

Dr. Charles Summers Robinson visited Glen Lake during a University of Michigan summer field trip to Camp Davis in Burdickville sometime between 1902 and 1908. He and fellow engineering students lived in tents and practiced the technical skills they were taught in class, such as surveying and monitoring streams. Robinson returned to Glen Lake in 1921 and purchased all fourteen lots in a subdivision named Glen Lake Country Club Resort, platted by George Johnson on the east side of the lake below the Glen Lake Country Club. His wife Florence (Sherwood) Robinson was upset about borrowing $1000 from Empire National Bank to buy 1000 feet of frontage as at that time they had four children and her husband's salary as head of the Experimental Chemistry Department at Michigan State Agricultural College was $2400 per year. She must have begun to feel better when Robinson sold the first lot for $600. He sold lots to several friends: Ove Jensen, a chemist; Zeland and Peter Goodell; and Henry Darlington, a botany professor at Michigan State Agricultural College. Ove Jensen designed and built neighbor Darlington's cottage in 1926.

The next documented visit the Robinsons made was in 1924 when they were picked up at the train station in Solon and stayed at Dunn's Farm. They supervised the construction of their two-story cottage that the contractor placed beside the old road where he dropped the lumber, rather than where Florence wished nearer to the water. Mrs. Robinson had also envisioned a formal dining room,

which did not happen. So, being inventive and artistic, she built wood curtains and painted them with her daughter Carolyn's paints. She also painted trees, a clock and a vase on the walls between the studs. The walls in one bedroom are painted with large polka dots by Libby Robinson, son Charles' wife. When electricity arrived in the early 1930s, the composting toilet was replaced but the pump and stove remained. Furnishings were rejects from their downstate home. Their maternal grandmother's piano, inherited in 1930, transformed the cottage into a center for music and a good excuse for a party. Many a merry game of hide-and-seek and tag ensued through the open second floor rafters above the bedroom walls.

The family cherished their Glen Lake vacations. They became friends with the Dunns. Mrs. Robinson and Mrs. Sarah (Dunn) Johnson organized children's activities on their side of the lake. As the Robinsons did not own a car, traveling here was difficult until they inherited grandfather's Dodge open touring car in 1927. The Robinson's old wooden row boat with double oarlocks was their means of transportation to Dunn's Farm for ice and milk and to John Holden's store in Burdickville for groceries where they had a charge account they paid monthly. Robinson rigged a pulley system to pull the boat to shore when ready for use. He also built a raft out of 55-gallon barrels which served as a community dock. Vacations were spent together outdoors: rowing across the lake, walking around it, taking trips to the Dunes and going to the outdoor movies. Cottage life revolved around the porch where they ate their meals, played games and where son Charles slept. Summer of 1935, Charles caddied and maintained the golf course greens behind their cottage.

The cottage, named *Robinson's Last Resort* by Charles in 1940, remains in the family in near original condition. A second cottage built in 1948 near the water's edge assured that the older generation always had a place to stay when the younger family visited.

1924

CHARLES AND FLORENCE ROBINSON COTTAGE

COTTAGE: Two-story wood frame, farm-style home clad with Dutch-lap siding originally painted battleship grey, six-light sash windows

INTERIOR: Walls are exposed studs and rafters; first floor contains a sitting porch, living room and kitchen; second floor has three bedrooms and a screened sleeping porch which has been glassed in; attached ice house turned into a fifth bedroom

FRONTAGE: 200 feet

MAP LOCATION: L7, #73

HOBLET • DENNISON COTTAGE

Main cottage

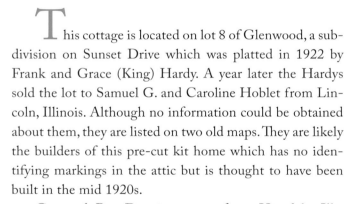

Bunkhouse

This cottage is located on lot 8 of Glenwood, a subdivision on Sunset Drive which was platted in 1922 by Frank and Grace (King) Hardy. A year later the Hardys sold the lot to Samuel G. and Caroline Hoblet from Lincoln, Illinois. Although no information could be obtained about them, they are listed on two old maps. They are likely the builders of this pre-cut kit home which has no identifying markings in the attic but is thought to have been built in the mid 1920s.

Gus and Bea Dennison were from Hinsdale, Illinois, and bought the cottage in the late 1940s after Jay and Rachel Hench of Hinsdale owned it for a short period of time. Gus and Jay were close friends from home and fished together on Glen Lake. As the Dennison and Hench families stayed here all summer, they participated in many activities together. After Gus died in 1967, his son and daughter inherited and rented out the cottage.

Horace H., Jr. and Jane Cobb of Hinsdale, Illinois, were looking for a place to rent and were told about Dennison's cottage by Kay (Hench) Whitney. When they inquired, they found out that the family had decided to sell. In 1972, the Cobbs purchased it furnished, sight unseen, and were pleasantly surprised and charmed by the cottage and its original wicker furniture. Cobb installed wood interior siding over the bare studs which retained the original numbering on the boards. The numbering, showing how the boards were to be constructed, is still visible on the porch. They added a dining area off the kitchen to the back but have kept the integrity of the original design of the cottage intact. With this same sensitivity to maintaining the cottage's original architectural style, they added a separate cottage containing the master bedroom suite which is connected by an outside covered walk.

Bunkhouse

Mid-1920s

Samuel and Caroline Hoblet • Gus and Bea Dennison Cottage

Description: One-story wood frame kit cottage with a rounded edge lap-siding originally painted cream with green trim

Interior: Living/dining room with fieldstone chimney, kitchen, two bedrooms, front porch the length of the cottage retains the original open stud construction

Addition: Dining area off kitchen, master bedroom suite built with similar architectural style in a separate cottage addition connected by a walkway

Outbuildings: Double-car garage, bunkhouse with living area, kitchen, double bunk beds

Frontage: 125 feet

Map Location: G5, #143

LERCHEN COTTAGE

George and Mary Mason of Cedar, Michigan, sold this property in 1925 to Alfred T. and Emma A. (Walz) Lerchen from Detroit where Alfred was in real estate. The Lerchens saw a cottage they liked in Leelanau County and asked permission to copy it. This was granted provided they change something, so they made it a mirror image. The cottage design takes after a New England Meeting House with a lofty interior and is a story and a half. The main room with fieldstone fireplace and loft has a gambrel roof line with Celotex between the wood rafters. Except for the maple flooring, all of the interior wood is Douglas-fir which was harvested and milled in Frankfort, Michigan, and shipped by boat to Glen Haven as documented on an original shipping tag.

The Lerchen cottage, boathouse and garage were built in 1925 on an acre of land on the northeast shore of Glen Lake. The cottage was well built and is now used as a guest-house. The concrete foundation, 10' x 40' concrete porch and garage floor with dog footprints show no cracks or repairs. The fieldstone foundation and chimney have never needed tuck-pointing.

The cottage's integrity has remained intact along with the original double-drain porcelain kitchen sink with grease disposal drain below, bathroom sink and bathtub. Many of the original furnishings also remain, including the grand piano that their only child Mary played, Indiana hickory rockers and table, and wicker chair and desk on the porch.

Mr. Lerchen who died in 1945, and Mrs. Lerchen (d.1956) passed the property to their daughter Mary, a music teacher in the Detroit school system. Mary married Charles Baker later in life and did not have children. Following his retirement and after suffering a stroke, Charles was not able to manage stairs so they built a house on M-109 on the way to Glen Haven. They would return by car to watch sunsets from their lake property.

1925

ALFRED AND EMMA LERCHEN COTTAGE

COTTAGE: One-and-a-half-story wood frame New England Meeting House style clad with cedar shingles

INTERIOR: Main room with loft, cut-fieldstone fireplace, dining room, kitchen and two bedrooms

1970S RENOVATION: Replaced two layers of asphalt shingles and original shake roof with cedar-shake roof

1980S UPDATES: Three skylights, arched window above the kitchen sink, Jutel stove insert in the fireplace, and an extended roofline over the front porch

OUTBUILDINGS: Single-stall garage with utility room and adjacent elaborate underground system designed to pipe gas to the cottage for the stove and lanterns; two-story boathouse with painted lap-siding built into the hill with boat storage below and large open screened room above

1949 BOATHOUSE RENOVATION: By Kieft and Dorsey to create two bedrooms, seating area and Pullman kitchen upstairs; wood stringers, rollers and an electric winch downstairs

1990 REPLACEMENT: Dr. Richard Green, a dentist from Hinsdale, Illinois, and his wife Linda, built a home on the site of the boathouse designed by Bob Lange of Leland, Michigan.

PROPERTY: One acre of land with lake frontage owned by William and Peggy Dotterweich since 1998

MAP LOCATION: L6, #90

WILSON • FETZER COTTAGE

George R. and A. Hazel (Thorne) Wilson first stayed at Gregory's Tonawathya and registered a gas boat on Glen Lake in 1922. They purchased property from the Gregorys and had built this cottage by 1925. It was designed early in the career of R. Harold Zook who designed a number of Tudor and Cotswold style cottages with thatched roofs in Hinsdale, Illinois, and the western suburbs of Chicago. Zook was known for incorporating chevron patterns, cathedral beams, curved staircases and, in a quarter of his favored residences, he incorporated his signature spider web design. This wonderful vacation home has several distinctive Zook details: fireplace bricks laid in a chevron pattern, shutters, window boxes and a Dutch door entrance with handwrought metal hinges. It originally contained a leaded glass spider web window at the ceiling line toward the lake. The 24' x 26' living/dining room has a high vaulted and beamed ceiling with a tapered split-fieldstone fireplace with brick inlays. A screened porch faces the lake. There were originally two screened sleeping porches on either side and two dressing rooms, later converted to bedrooms.

Later in his business career as an advertising manager, Mr. Wilson worked for Wade Fetzer and was responsible, along with William Burr, for the Fetzers coming to Glen Lake. Mr. Wilson lived his entire life in Hinsdale and was active at Union Church and a Director of the Chicago Congregational Union. The Wilsons had five children, George, Jr., Rev. R. Norris, Charlotte (Pratt), Barbara (Noyes) and Jean. After Mr. Wilson's death the cottage was sold in 1947 to the Fetzers who owned the adjacent property. Mrs. Fetzer had the spider web window removed because there were more than "enough spider webs in the cottage." The cottage was placed in the family corporation and retains its original integrity.

CIRCA 1925

GEORGE AND HAZEL WILSON • WADE AND MARGARET FETZER COTTAGE

ARCHITECT: Roscoe Harold Zook of Hinsdale, Ilinois

COTTAGE: One-story wood frame cottage clad with brown painted wide lap-siding, tapered cut-fieldstone chimney with brick inlaid chevron pattern, shutters, Dutch-door entrance with handwrought metal hinges, six-light casement windows

INTERIOR: Wide knotty-cedar tongue-and-groove walls, Douglas-fir floors, high vaulted and beamed living room ceiling, kitchen, four bedrooms, three bathrooms and screened front porch

OUTBUILDINGS: Garage with bunkbeds for overflow guests has been taken down, one-room yellow cottage used by Mrs. Wilson after her husband passed away

FRONTAGE: 200 feet

MAP LOCATION: G6, #159

COLLINGS • SIMPSON/DUNSCOMBE COTTAGE

1926

HELEN S. COLLINGS • JEAN SIMPSON, CHARLES AND FERNIE DUNSCOMBE COTTAGE

COTTAGE: One-story wood frame cottage clad with Dutch-lap siding

INTERIOR: Large front porch, living/dining room, kitchen, three bedrooms; interior walls of natural colored Celotex

1953 ADDITION: Enlarged the kitchen, added a dining room and basement

OUTBUILDINGS: Guest cottage (later moved to become a bedroom addition), beach house on the lake side of the road

FRONTAGE: 200 feet

MAP LOCATION: F6, #163

Desiring a change from renting in Omena, Michigan, Helen (Spiece) Collings decided to build a cottage on a lake and friends recommended she drive over to see Glen Lake. This was after the death of her younger son Robert and divorce from John Henry Beckett Collings, owner of a Detroit insurance company. She purchased a lot adjacent to Tonawathya on the hill side of M-22 on the west shore of Glen Lake in 1926 and began construction of a cottage with a grand 50-foot porch across the front. The night before she was scheduled to move her furniture into the cottage, it burned to the ground leaving only the stone chimney. When Mrs. Collings arrived she discovered that not only had the cottage burned down, but that all of the furniture–delivered a day early–had been destroyed in the fire, as well. She rebuilt it but did not live there many years. Her son John Barton remembers enjoying sleeping in the beach house when they had guests, riding his bicycle and meeting children his age. He became lifelong friends

with the Johnson family who included him in their family activities. In 1929 Mrs. Collings built another cottage on Sunset Drive and then married a family friend, Fletcher Hemstead Field, owner of a manufacturing business.

Helen offered her first cottage for rent to Detroit-area friends, Jean (Hamilton) Simpson and her only child, daughter Fernie and son-in law, Charles Dunscombe, who purchased it a year later. Jean was the widow of Walter Simpson, who founded the H.S.H. Lunch Company, a Ford Motor Company caterer. The Dunscombes and their three children Charles, Ian and Billie (Kremer), were an active, fun-loving family and the cottage became a center for their children and friends. Picnics, games on the porch, and horseback riding were daily summer-long activities. They had a large Chris-Craft and were known to water ski at night holding torches. Their father never complained about the high monthly charges for gas at Ralston's Marina. The cottage remains in the family.

RAINES COTTAGE *(Hill Cottage, Glen Glorious)*

This cottage was built in 1927 by the Gregorys, owners of Tonawathya Resort, and was referred to as the *Hill Cottage* as it was behind the Inn and up the hill. Like many of their cottages, the Gregorys built it for family rental. It was rented for many years by Phillip and Lillian Swartz, missionaries from Indiana, and then by the Addoms family of Beloit, Wisconsin, who later purchased a cottage from the Beatty family to the south of the inn. The Symonds family of Hinsdale, Illinois, rented it for several years before they purchased the Hench cottage also to the south.

The cottage takes its name from the family that rented it one summer and made it their summer home. Bishop Richard Campbell and Lucille (Arnold) Raines bought it in 1949 from Asa Case who had purchased Tonawathya. At the time, the Raines' lived in Indianapolis, Indiana, where he was Bishop of the United Methodist Church and learned about Glen Lake from friends. The Raines' spent several weeks every summer at the cottage with their children, Rose, Bob, Dick and John. The three brothers, became ordained Methodist ministers, and two became college teachers. Their father was known for taking charge of critter control for the area by relocating the porcupines to Lake Michigan. The Raines family renamed the cottage *Glen Glorious* after they discovered the name carved by the original builders on a stone platform below the porch.

The Raines children remember dressing up for the formal Sunday dinner at the Inn when lobster bisque was ladled from a silver tureen. They also recall the Sunday evening hymn sings at the Glen Lake Yacht Club. They cherish Glen Lake and their neighbors with whom they have shared a common dock since 1949. The cottage remains in the family in much the original condition.

1927

RICHARD AND LUCILLE RAINES COTTAGE
(Hill Cottage, Glen Glorious)
COTTAGE: One-story wood frame clad with wide Dutch-lap siding

INTERIOR: Beaded board and exposed studs; paneled living room, front porch, dining room, kitchen, four linked bedrooms, two of them sleeping porches

OUTBUILDINGS: Two guest cottages built in 1950s *(Upper Room)* and 1965 *(Last Resort)*, for overflow guests and family

FRONTAGE: 50 foot with shared dock and easement

MAP LOCATION: F6, not numbered

White • Schilling Cottage

1927

White • Schilling Cottage

Interior: Originally wood frame, one bedroom

Three Additions: First, added living room with fieldstone fireplace, cedar walls and ceiling, Douglas-fir floors and two bedrooms; later additions in 1948 and 1959 added three bedrooms, updated and winterized

Outbuildings: 1960s one car garage with office/darkroom, garage/boat storage near the road moved next to the cottage

Frontage: 205 feet

Map Location: J4, #121

Dr. Clara Hooper, who built the Glen Eden Resort in the early 1920s, built this one-bedroom cottage in 1927 and used it to house overflow resort guests. When Dr. Hooper's daughter, Juanita Tracy, inherited it she added two bedrooms and a living room with a fieldstone fireplace built of very large and small stones. After her husband died, she sold the cottage to Kirk and Felise White of Owosso, Michigan.

James C. White (not related to Kirk White) and his wife Vera (Wynkoop) bought the cottage in 1948, after having built one several lots away (See Map Location I4, #127). His family founded and named Solon, Michigan. They owned and operated sawmills on the mainland as well as at Crescent on North Manitou Island. The family later settled in Kingsport, Tennessee, where Mr. White became a director of Eastman Kodak Company and President of Tennessee Eastman Corporation. They had four children: Dorothy (Edwards), Ralph James, Andrew John and Barbara (Schilling). The family loved Glen Lake and continued to vacation here while living in Tennessee.

George T. Schilling, then of Hinsdale, Illinois, and Barbara Jean White met at Dunn's Farm on Glen Lake on her sixteenth birthday in 1937. George's parents, George A. and Ruth T. Schilling, first came to Glen Lake in 1928 from Detroit where Mr. Schilling was with the S.S. Kresge Company (later K-Mart). They had three children: George, Nancy, and Richard. George and Barbara were married in 1942 and had three children, Carolyn (Gery), George and Martha. When they purchased the cottage in 1959 they built an addition, further adding to its charm. Later, George and his father helped organize the Citizens Council of Sleeping Bear Dunes National Lakeshore. When George retired from his law practice in 1978, they moved from West Lafayette, Indiana, to Glen Lake. They sold the property in 2005 and returned to Indiana.

JOHNSON COTTAGE

Brother and sister Robert and Catherine Ambrosius were among the earliest Glen Lake summer resorters, arriving by boat from Chicago to Glen Haven in the early 1900s in search of relief from hay fever and allergies that plagued Robert. He was a cellist with the Chicago Symphony and Chicago Opera Company. They came with their brother's child, Marie Marjorie, and stayed at Little Traverse Lake. They traveled around the lakes by horse and buggy looking for a place to build, choosing to purchase from the Dorsey Family on Little Glen. Marie's mother had died in about 1905 when Marie was six years old. Her father Hermann Zacharius Ambrosius was a wealthy financial investor with Spires and Company in New York City but was unable to raise her. He sent her to Chicago to live with his unmarried brother and sister who sent her

to school at Sacred Heart Convent. Marie began studying piano early and her father bought her a Steinway. He remarried and had more children. Upon his death in 1916, Marie inherited gold bonds. A few years later she used this inheritance to purchase at least 1200 feet of frontage on the west shore of Glen Lake, just north of Gregory's Tonawathya Resort on property having belonged earlier to Dr. William Walker.

Marie had met and fallen in love with Anthony Angarola, an artist whose brother was a cello pupil of her uncle Robert. Angarola was a talented impressionist oil painter who taught at the Art Institute of Chicago. Her aunt and uncle tried to interfere with the relationship but Anthony visited her at the lake, staying with their next door neighbors the Dorseys. He painted a small oil painting of their

The children gathered the stones for the fieldstone chimney. A narrow screened porch with canvas awnings was added along with a narrow railing-less staircase to the second floor. It was to serve as a temporary residence until a larger cottage could be built, but the Depression changed those plans. On either end of the cottage a sleeping porch and kitchen were added. There was a wood cook stove and a hole in the floor which served as a cooler until an icebox was installed. Although the family had live-in help in Chicago, they did not bring them to the lake. The family drove two cars to the lake, a Jewett and a Paige.

All of Marie's children were musical: Yvonne Angarola (Daly) played the piano, taught music in Pennsylvania and teaches now in the Glen Lake home studio she built in 1991; Richard Angarola, a cellist and actor, moved to California and was a movie actor; Hilda Johnson (Zierk) was a violinist and taught in Wisconsin; Frances Johnson (Baad) was a clarinetist, taught clarinet and played in the Battle Creek Symphony; Harvey Johnson is a dentist in St. Joseph, Michigan; Robert is an orthodontist in California. The cottage remains in the family and has retained its original integrity and some of the original furnishings.

home, *Elizabeth House*. Marie and Anthony eloped and had two children, Yvonne (Daly) and Richard. Angarola took teaching positions at the Kansas City Art School and the Art Institute of Minneapolis and received a two-year Guggenheim fellowship to paint in France and Italy in 1927. Meanwhile Mrs. Angarola continued her piano studies with Paulo Gallico in New York City. By 1924 she had divorced Angarola at her aunt and uncle's encouragement and married her physician, Dr. Harvey C. Johnson, a surgeon at Grant Hospital in Chicago. She was a concert pianist and each year brought a piano with her to the lake which she would leave up here, often donating them. She was one of the first women to drive in northern Michigan.

In 1927 the Johnsons returned to Glen Lake and stayed at Ray's Resort while they rebuilt a boathouse measuring 14 ' x 24' that they had moved across the ice from Burdickville several years before. It rested on wood piers.

1927

HARVEY AND MARIE JOHNSON COTTAGE

BUILDER: Frank Petrosky and Carl A. Oleson, Glen Arbor, Michigan

COTTAGE: Two-story wood frame construction with wide Dutch-lap siding

INTERIOR: Living room with fieldstone fireplace, kitchen and two porches; upstairs two open bedrooms with open rafters and stud walls which are written on by visiting friends and relatives

FRONTAGE: 100 feet

MAP LOCATION: G5, #146

Lott Cottage

Antone L. Lott, the owner of Motor Products in Detroit, and his wife Neville (Ensor) purchased 1,000 feet on the north shore of Glen Lake in 1928 from Raymond and Dorothy Baxter. Mrs. Lott influenced the placement of the cottage far back from the lake as she preferred not to hear her sons, Tom, George, Bill and Jack, and finally daughter Marion at the beach. The family entertained large groups of friends, who sometimes dined on prime rib roasts prepared by the Detroit Athletic Club sent by train to Traverse City. The great room still contains a baby grand piano that held a large bouquet of gladiolas, a juke box, game and card tables and bar. A tennis court and gazebo were placed between the cottage and the lake.

Since Mrs. Lott did not like to smell food cooking, a separate cottage was built for the kitchen, dining room and the help. Later a local couple Henry and Rose cooked and served the family their evening meals which always ended with tasty pies, most often lemon.

The Lott "boys," who were in their later teens when the cottage was built, were known locally for being on the wild side, driving fast boats and cars. One legend has it that they attempted to deliver a new aluminum Lincoln from Detroit to the cottage and wrecked it on the way. The second attempted delivery ended in the same condition. Another legend was that they dated many Traverse City Cherry Festival Queens and bragged about it into old age. In addition to a sailboat, they owned a classic 22-foot Chris-Craft, which they ran long and hard, sometimes pulling six or seven skiers at once.

In 1972 Wade III and Bev Fetzer of Glencoe, Illinois, purchased the property from the Lott family estate. Fetzer summered at his family's cottage on the west side of Glen Lake but wanted to build a new home of his own closer to the water. This allowed them to keep these cottages virtually intact for family and guests. The cottage was named *The Wing*.

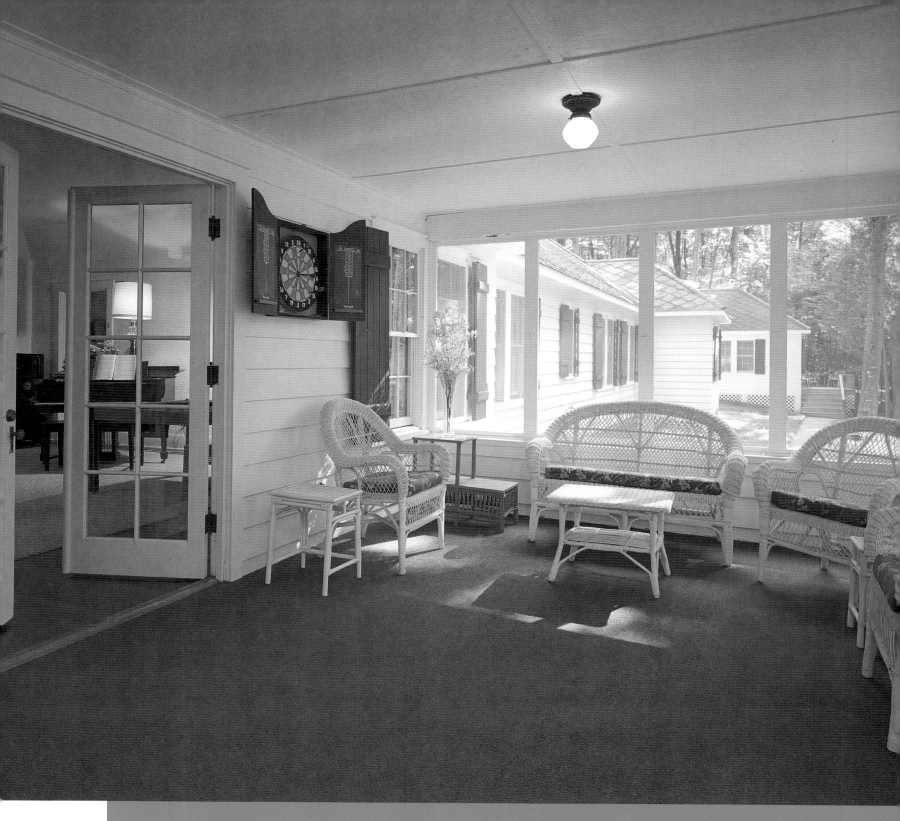

1928

ANTONE AND NEVILLE LOTT COTTAGE

COTTAGE: Two one-story wood frame cottages (main cottage and kitchen annex) clad with wide lap-siding painted white with green trim; double-hung, double six-light windows; terra cotta-colored large octagonal shaped slate tile roof; two-car garage under the cottage

INTERIOR MAIN COTTAGE: Great room with cut-stone fireplace, screened front porch, entry room, long halls with five bedrooms, the back bedroom with four beds for the boys named the "Kennel", Douglas-fir floors, Celotex walls and ceilings

INTERIOR KITCHEN ANNEX: Dining room, kitchen, two bedrooms for the help, Celotex walls and ceilings

OUTBUILDING: Gazebo by the lake

LANDSCAPE FEATURES: Tennis court, extensive myrtle ground cover, and rock-lined path to the lake

FRONTAGE: 400 of the original 1000 front feet remain

MAP LOCATION: I4, #130

LANPHIER COTTAGE *(Grey Gables)*

Grey Gables sits on the bluff along the northeast side of Glen Lake on Dunn's Farm Road. The grey cedar-shake cottage with cut fieldstone chimney was built by Robert Carr Lanphier, Sr. of Springfield, Illinois, in 1928. Mr. Lanphier was the founder and president of the Sangamo Electric Company which produced electric meters and time switches. He and his wife Bertha (Oliver) and children, Robert Jr., Charles and Margaret (Wangren) had been staying at Gregory's Tonawathya Resort for a few years before purchasing next door to his first cousin, Dr. Charles Lanphier Patton. They purchased 500 feet, including a small white cottage, from Howard and Orpha (Fralick) Burfiend of Port Oneida, Michigan.

Pleased with the design for their Springfield home, the Lanphiers asked Henry and George Helmle to design their two-story Glen Lake cottage as well. Helmle and

Helmle had also designed Patton's cottage and several cottages for other Springfield summer residents in Northport and on Old Mission Peninsula. After returning from a 1927 summer vacation in Europe, they broke ground for their grand cottage with a 40' x 24' living room. The building crew camped in tents on the property and went home on the weekends. The Lanphiers stayed in the little white cottage during construction. This was later used as a guest house.

The family came to Glen Lake to escape Springfield's heat and to be with family and for a social change. They drove two cars to the lake which was a trip of several days, sometimes broken up by a few days in Chicago. A Wednesday social activity for the women was driving to Traverse City, accompanied by their cooks who dropped them at the Park Place Hotel, for lunch and visiting with other Spring-

field friends summering in the area, while the help did the shopping. The families' servants met as well in Traverse City on their day off.

A boathouse, with living quarters on the second floor, was added in 1937, just north of a swampy, boggy area "infested with big snakes." In the early 1960s a large turn-around channel was dredged from the shoal and the sand placed in this boggy area. In 1967, a new tennis court was built on this lake sand, replacing the original tennis court built on the east side of Dunn's Farm Road. Today this area is the center of activities, lunches and evening cook-outs. These informal events have replaced the served meals of the first generation.

Lanphier's daughter Margaret remembers aquaplaning, the grand-daddy of skis, behind the Chris-Craft. Five generations share fond memories of "Glen Lake Days" playing tennis, sailing, boating, water skiing, swimming, tribal camp fires, climbing the dunes, and playing on Lake Michigan beaches. After Robert Carr Sr.'s death, Mrs. Lanphier vacationed in Harbor Springs to be near friends. The cottage remains in the family virtually unchanged. A major addition in 2005, designed by Traverse City architect Ken Richmond and built by Biggs Construction, has maintained the integrity of original design and cottage function.

1938 Grey Gables birthday celebration
(Lanphier Family Collection)

1938 Lanphier family on the porch
(Lanphier Family Collection)

1928

ROBERT AND BERTHA LANPHIER COTTAGE *(Grey Gables)*

ARCHITECT: Henry and George Helmle of Helmle and Helmle, Springfield, Illinois

BUILDER: Frank Plamondon, Lake Leelanau, Michigan

COTTAGE: Two-story wood frame cottage sided with grey painted cedar shakes

INTERIOR: Knotty-pine interior, large living room with cut-fieldstone fireplace, porch facing the lake, dining room, kitchen and pantry; a stairwell with a cut-out arrow design in the wood balustrade and a half-bath on the landing, four upstairs bedrooms

OUTBUILDINGS: Attached garage with adjacent quarters for live-in help was torn down for 2005 addition; boathouse built 1937 with second story two bedroom living quarters; two-story white cottage sold in 1949 with 100 feet; new three-bedroom winterized home built to house older generation in 1971

FRONTAGE: 500 feet

MAP LOCATION: L5, #98

FETZER COTTAGE *(Hill House)*

Wade and Margaret (Spillman) Fetzer of Hinsdale, Illinois, had been vacationing in Harbor Springs, Michigan, until the doctors recommended their daughter Mary Jane be kept out of Chicago all summer to help alleviate her childhood asthma. Friends from Hinsdale, George and Hazel Wilson, recommended Gregory's Tonawathya on the west shore of Glen Lake. In 1927 after one summer at the resort, the Fetzers purchased a 300-foot lot from the Gregorys to build a cottage for their family. Their children were John Clark, Wade Jr., Margaret (Sherman) and Mary Jane (Bryant).

Wade gave his wife the job of planning and overseeing the building of the cottage over the winter of 1927. She wanted it to look like a chalet with cross ventilation, closet space in the bedrooms, and lots of room for family and friends. The cottage was to be sited on the hill across the road with a good view of the lake. Chicago architect Vernon Watson of Tallmadge and Watson, a firm known for arts and crafts design, turned her penciled sketch into blueprints.

In early June 1928, Mrs. Fetzer returned with her mother, daughter Mary Jane, and their Swedish chauffeur August Anderson and stayed at the Gregory's. She oversaw the cottage's construction from her perch on a sawhorse. The builders, under Frank Plamondon, were accomplished craftsman. The stonemason who built the fireplace inquired if he should build it as designed or so that it would work. The furniture, which Mrs. Fetzer had purchased on closeout at Marshall Fields the winter before and had shipped to Glen Haven via the *Manitou*, was being stored in the Cannery. Mid-construction, the wicker furniture and Simmons metal bedroom furniture had to be moved as the

cannery was needed for the cherry season. Since the stairway had not been built, local trucker Martin Egeler raised the furniture piece by piece to the attic using a pulley.

The cottage has twelve rooms with a grand two-story 30' by 24' living room. It was the first cottage around the lake to have indoor plumbing. Electricity became available a year later. External and internal walls were built with California redwood, which was spotted by Watson when he accompanied Fetzer and Plamondon to Traverse City to select the building materials. Watson recommended using the redwood, mistakenly dropped in Traverse City en route to Chicago. Mr. Fetzer, an insurance executive with W.A. Alexander and Company of Chicago, was later pleased to find out that redwood was fire resistant and thus reduced his insurance rates.

Social activity, as documented in the guest book, began August 1, 1928, with a housewarming for 40 friends and new neighbors who became lifelong friends. Chairs were scarce, so guests sat on the floor enjoying the feast prepared by Hinsdale caterers. The family also enjoyed many hours on the lake in their chauffeur-driven Chris-Craft and their sailboat built by Ray Greene of Glen Lake. Fetzer liked music and was known to sing at family functions and while boating.

Fetzer placed the cottage in a family corporation that maintains it virtually unchanged for the now-extended family.

Mary Jane sitting on the porch
(Fetzer Family Collection)

Spirit of Wade Fetzer keeping an eye on *Hill House (Cynthia Dougal)*

1928

WADE AND MARGARET FETZER COTTAGE *(Hill House)*

ARCHITECT: Vernon S. Watson of Tallmadge and Watson, Chicago, Illinois

BUILDER: Frank Plamondon, Lake Leelanau, Michigan

COTTAGE: Two-story large wood frame cottage clad in redwood wide lap-siding, open porch with flared wood base, living room windows set in tall arched pattern

INTERIOR: Two-story living room with balcony and large tapered cut-fieldstone chimney; first floor dining room, kitchen, pantry, ping pong room, two bedrooms; second floor four bedrooms with buff colored Celotex walls and ceilings; basement

OUTBUILDINGS: Boathouse with dressing rooms

LANDSCAPE FEATURE: Stone-lined stairs leading down the hill to the road, shuffleboard court

FRONTAGE: 300 feet

MAP LOCATION: F6, #154

BURR • PRATT COTTAGE

William B. and Helen S. (Jennings) Burr moved to Hinsdale, Illinois, in 1910 to facilitate William's commute on the Burlington Railroad to a brokerage firm in downtown Chicago where he worked. He was an active community leader and chaired the building of the Hinsdale Memorial Building. After coming to Glen Lake and staying at Gregory's, the Burrs purchased 200 feet of frontage from them on the west shore in 1925. They built a grand two-story cottage in 1929 along with a boathouse and servants quarters/garage. The outbuildings were later remodeled into guest cottages.

The Burrs and their five children, Mary Jane (Barton), Phoebe, Wallace and twins John and Priscilla, were friends with the other families from Hinsdale who vacationed at Gregory's. William loved fishing with his friends and seemed to love Glen Lake most of all. Within the ten years after William passed away, from 1945 to 1955, the cottage passed through three different owners: Weldon and Jessie Lutey, William Dennis, Harold and Lucille Cunningham.

Dana W. and Amanda L. Pratt bought the cottage in 1955 and named it *The Pines*. They lived in Hamilton, Ohio, where he was a sales executive with Champion Paper, but were originally from Hinsdale. They first came to Glen Lake to stay with friends at Salisbury cottages on Little Glen. The cottage remained in the family for forty-three years, first inherited by their son and then their grandchildren, Dana II, Marilynn, Nancy and William. When all extended family members were staying in the three cottages, dinners were held in shifts at the long dining room table in the lodge. Children were fed first, followed by adults. The Pratt children held summer jobs on Glen Lake, working at Seebergers, Old Orchard Inn and the Glen Lake Yacht Club. Their years on Glen Lake were sacred and provided many wonderful memories. The cottage was sold in 1998 to Jeffrey and Phyllis Totten of Washington, DC.

1929

WILLIAM AND HELEN BURR •
DANA AND AMANDA PRATT COTTAGE

COTTAGE: Two-story wood frame cottage clad
in wide, painted lap-siding with mullioned casement windows

INTERIOR: Large two-story living room with brick fireplace,
porch facing the lake, kitchen and two bedrooms on the first
floor; upstairs four bedrooms entered off the L-shaped balcony
with sinks in each; cedar wide-wood planking with beaded
board ceilings; Douglas-fir floors

2000 REMODELING AND UPDATING: Painted beaded board
ceilings, removed bedroom sinks and redecorated; 2006
built new decking and stairs to the lake

OUTBUILDINGS: Three-story guest cottage no longer part
of property after 1996 property split; garage/servant's
quarters/guest cottage torn down in 1996

FRONTAGE: 200 feet (100 feet after lot split in 1996)

MAP LOCATION: G6, not numbered

GOODNOW • BRADY COTTAGE *(Glen Gables)*

The cottage was built in 1929 by the E.W. Goodnows and their two children who were friends of Glen Lake neighbors, Williston and Ethelyn Keen. Some ten years later the Goodnows were involved in a fatal car accident on their way to Glen Lake and as a result felt unable to continue coming to the lake.

Harold and Madeline (Keller) Brady and their three daughters, Betty (Mooney, Strobel), Donelda (Kuebler) and Carol (Noel), were from Flint, Michigan, and had heard about Glen Lake from the 1934 *National Geographic* article touting it as one of the most beautiful lakes in the world. They rented for two years from the Salisburys on Little Glen. While walking down the road, which at that time ran in front of the cottage, they noticed a for sale sign.

The Bradys purchased the cottage for $4000 in 1944. The interior had not been completed and there was an inside water pump. Harold worked for General Motors and when they stopped making the old Woody station wagons,

he acquired a lot of the wood. He finished it, cut it into pieces and nailed it inside all of the rooms of the cottage. When the land in back became available, they purchased it and cut a drive through as by then the road had been moved behind the cottage.

The Bradys loved nature and the surrounding trees. Although they later moved to Cleveland, they came up every chance they could, even if only for a weekend. The more people that visited the more fun they had. Summer foods like berries and fresh corn tasted better at the lake than anywhere else. When they arrived they raced to see who could get into the hammock first and then visited Rader's gift shop to see what new goodies had arrived. The Bradys were active members of the Noontiders, an organization dedicated to the betterment of the area. The cottage which remains in the family was restored in 2004 to its 1940s grandeur by Brady's granddaughter Jennifer Glassman and her husband Rick.

1929

E.W. Goodnow • Harold and Madeline Brady Cottage *(Glen Gables)*

Cottage: Two-story wood frame cottage clad with wide lap-siding, eight-light casement windows

Interior: Living room with fieldstone fireplace, dining room, kitchen, front porch, three upstairs bedrooms

2003–2004 Restoration: Replaced acoustic tile ceilings with painted beaded board

Outbuilding: Garage had a workshop added in the mid-1940s

Frontage: 100 feet

Map Location: B7, #206

(Brady Family Collection)

KEEN • MERCER LOG COTTAGE

Howard A. Keen was a Detroit commercial artist who was commissioned to do an ad for a Wisconsin log company. As payment, he received a one-room log kit cottage which was delivered to Glen Haven in 1929. His wife Margaret (Nesbitt) called her favorite aunt and uncle, Isabel (Nesbitt) and Henry C.L. Forler, a Detroit attorney, asking permission to place it on their lot on the west shore of Little Glen Lake. His parents, Williston and Ethelyn Keen, had a summer cottage on the adjacent lot. By 1939, Howard was divorced from Margaret and dying of tuberculosis, the result of having been gassed in World War I. He spent his last summer alive sleeping on the porch of his beloved cabin, being taken food by Edith, his parent's maid.

Margaret did not visit for many years until after she married Edwin J. Mercer, a lawyer from Detroit, who had served during World War II. Their only child, then nine year-old Gay (Budinger), remembers bushwhacking their way through the brush from the old two-track road between the cottage and the lake in order to reach the cabin in 1946. Margaret and Edwin talked Forler's daughter and son-in-law, Joseph

and Kay (Forler) Wright, into coming up with their children Ann (Davey), Alan (Sara), and Betsy (Johnson) as well, and they stayed in tents until they built their own cottage next door in 1950.

The family compound included Williston and Ethelyn Keen's *Beach Knoll* to the south built in 1920 by C.A. Cable. The Keen grandchildren Barbara (Edward Collins), James (Jane) and Thomas (Barbara) were similar ages as the cousins and remain close. Most have returned to live in the area. Gay (Mercer) Budinger has fond memories of summers being a reprieve from the restrictions of the social life in Grosse Pointe, Michigan. Gay loved sleeping on the porch, often with her cousin Ann Wright (Davey). The cottage has had two additions which maintain its integrity and charm as compatible construction and materials were used. A few original shipping labels were found during a recent renovation. The cabin remains in the family furnished with cozy cottage furniture Margaret collected.

Cottage photo showing lantern from Good Harbor Settlement on post, 1939

(Keen Family Collection)

1929

HOWARD AND MARGARET KEEN •
EDWIN AND MARGARET MERCER
LOG COTTAGE

COTTAGE: One-room vertical cedar log kit cottage with built-in bunkbed, front and kitchen porch

1948 ADDITION: Built by Mr. Swallow of B. & L. Log and Lumber Company from Lake George, Michigan, who was building the Wright cottage next door at the same time; electric power added, window replaced with a Heatilator fireplace, one bedroom for Mercers, and one for Margaret's mother

1960 ADDITION: Kitchen and bathroom built by Schaub

FRONTAGE: 50 feet

Map Location: A7, #204

Margaret posing with gun at cabin entrance

(Budinger Family Collection)

Sherwood Shack

CIRCA 1930

Sherwood Shack

SHACK: One-story wood frame shack clad in lap-siding, drop shuttered windows

INTERIOR: Thought to originally have a living, dining, kitchen, bedroom and screened porch

BUNKHOUSE: One-room wood frame clad in lap siding with 4 bunk beds and pot belly stove reluctantly replaced by a guest house in 1985

FRONTAGE: 120 feet

MAP LOCATION: I4, #124

In 1930 Dr. Sherwood and his wife Katherine purchased this property on the north shore of Glen Lake from Clara Hooper of Glen Eden Hotel. As Dr. Hooper was from Toledo and owned the property on Fisher Point, many of the properties along that shoreline were purchased by people from the Toledo area. The Sherwoods were from Maumee where Dr. Sherwood was a dentist. They had a son named Duke, a well-built muscular young man who practiced his gymnastics on a rod between the trees. Katherine was athletic as well and canoed the Crystal River. The Sherwoods built a cottage and also two primitive structures, a shack and a bunkhouse. Katherine was also an artist and painted the inside of the *Sherwood Shack* exterior door. As there were hinged shutters covering the screen door and openings, it was it difficult to keep sand and the elements from coming inside.

Dr. Ernest and Martha Stefani, who also vacationed at Glen Eden, purchased the property in 1948. Ernest was a general surgeon in Detroit and enjoyed listening to Italian opera on his porch. Their only son Greg was a General Motors truck and bus engineer. Dr. and Mrs. Stefani had a brick fireplace built by a stonemason and hired Charles

Musil, a skilled carpenter who lived on the Crystal River, to finish the interior of *Sherwood Shack* with planed sawmill wood. The cottage has birdseye maple flooring which is unusual.

In 1965 the Stefanis decided to divide their property and sell the *Sherwood Shack* and bunk house. Webster Cook and his wife Betty heard from Jay Dutmers of Dunn's Farm that the property was for sale. The Cooks and their children Gary, Susan and Barbara became the third owners of the cottages. Webster's parents, Robert and Alice, had made their first trip to Glen Lake in 1920 after vacationing at Bay View, Petoskey, Michigan and had stayed at Ocker's Resort. On their next visit they were among the first guests to stay at Dunn's Farm. In 1924 they purchased a lot from the Dunns south of the resort and built a cottage with their friends the Brydges.

There may have been as many as ten changes to this cottage in its lifetime. It has managed to retain is small and cozy cottage feeling and integrity.

Stearns Cottage

Verlin Glen Stearns was the only son of Maude (Fisher) and Warren Stearns. Maude's parents were Francis "Frank" and Charlotte (Atkinson) Fisher and her grandparents were Glen Arbor pioneers, John and Harriet (McCarty) Fisher. Stearns married Katherine Elsie Williams in 1924 and they had two children, James Warren and Lois Jane. Stearns worked in an iron foundry in Muskegon and Katherine worked in a dry goods store. They moved to this area in the late 1930s, settling on family property north of Fisher Lake where the original Fisher farm was located. Prior to their move, Stearns had spent summers building a sawmill and fixing this cottage. When they moved here year-round, Stearns ran the sawmill that utilized some equipment from Frank Fisher's nearby mill on the Crystal River that Fisher ran until the 1930s.

When Stearns acquired this property, it included a one-room log cabin on the southeast side of the road where Fisher Lake flows into the Crystal River. As it took him some time to make it livable, the family stayed in a couple of shacks (one housed the bedrooms and the other the kitchen) across the water next to the Ralston's Marina, now Crystal River Marina. Stearns ceased his mill operation here in 1947 when he returned to work at the Muskegon iron foundry and was then sent to Cincinnati.

Lois Jane Stearns married Theodore J. Swierad and they have lived in the cottage since the early 1960s. With their daughter Christie and son-in-law, Thomas Schlosser, they purchased the property just to the north which included the Glen Arbor tea house. The tea house was Lyman Sheridan's original store which Frank Fisher had purchased and run before building a new one at the southeast corner of M-22 and CR-675. The tea house probably had been moved in the mid-1920s by Frank Fisher's daughter Myrtle for her daughter Edith Warnes. Both properties remain in the family.

DATE UNKNOWN

VERLIN AND KATHERINE STEARNS COTTAGE

COTTAGE: One-story one room log cottage with fieldstone fireplace and knotty wood boards fastened with square nails

INTERIOR: Living/dining/ kitchen, small bedroom, smoked fieldstone fireplace once had a stove, now permanently closed

1940S ADDITION: Stearns constructed a three bedroom addition using wood cut at his mill and with the help of his sawyers. Stearns constructed the fieldstone base that surrounds the cottage with help from his wife and children. He also covered the logs with vertical wood slabs

FRONTAGE: 66 feet

MAP LOCATION: J3, not numbered

BARTON COTTAGE

Enos M. and Mary Rust Barton had lived in Chicago, but moved to Sedgely House on Mr. Barton's dairy farm in 1907 in Hinsdale, Illinois. In 1911 following the birth of their fourth son, Mrs. Barton needed a more extended summer vacation. Business acquaintance Frank Gregory recommended his wife's resort on Glen Lake. The Bartons came to stay at Tonawathya and Mrs. Barton and their four sons, Malcolm, Evan, Gilbert and Wilfrid, continued to spend summers here. Mr. Barton, co-founder of Graybar Company which later became Western Electric, traveled back and forth from Chicago to Glen Haven by boat. After Mr. Barton's death in 1916, Mrs. Barton continued to bring her family to Glen Lake, eventually purchasing property from the Gregorys.

Mrs. Barton hired Chicago architect Earl Reed to design five small cottages, one for herself and each of her sons. Reed, who was at that time Director of the Department of Architecture at the Armour Institute of Technology (now the Illinois Institute of Technology), persuaded her to simplify her plans and build one two-story cottage.

When Mrs. Barton hired Frank Petrosky, who worked as a builder and handyman for the Gregorys, Reed's only stipulation was that he could read blueprints. Mrs. Barton had selected Petrosky as she wanted to help him get established as a builder. During construction she and Reed communicated by telegrams delivered to the Gregorys, the only telephone in the area. During the winter Petrosky prepared the cedar sapling fence with pointed ends on top which runs the length of the property. Following construction he continued as her caretaker.

Morning swims before breakfast became a summer-long tradition for the family and visitors. Mrs. Barton kept an active social calendar with friends from home and around the lake. The cottage, with most of its original furnishings, remains in the family.

1930

MARY R. BARTON COTTAGE

ARCHITECT: Earl Reed, Chicago

BUILDER: Frank Petrosky, Glen Arbor, Michigan

COTTAGE: Two-story frame cottage clad in painted wide lap siding, ornamental roof brackets, shutters with shutter dogs, six-light casement windows, and handwrought metal door hinges

INTERIOR: First floor living room with common brick fireplace and balcony, kitchen, three small bedrooms, screened porch with dining table; two upstairs medium-sized bedrooms with sinks, half bath on the stairway landing

LATE 1930s ADDITION: Extended the porch and wrapped it around the cottage to give access to the kitchen and connect it to the added housekeeper cottage

2001 ADDITION: Compatible remodeling to allow year-round residency added an attached garage; housekeeper cottage turned into a studio; indoor dining area added to the kitchen

OUTBUILDINGS: Screened dockhouse which stored boats in winter and had four beds for extra guests, garage built across M-22

LANDSCAPE FEATURE: Two stairways lead down the steep bluff to the lake,

FRONTAGE: 225 feet

MAP LOCATION: G5, #146

REA • WHITESIDE COTTAGE

Mrs. Inez Rea was first introduced to Glen Lake by Mildred Rea Whiteside, her daughter from her first marriage. Mrs. Whiteside's husband, Nathaniel Henry Whiteside Jr., had been coming to vacation at the Gregory's with his parents, Nathaniel H. and Marion Whiteside from Hinsdale, Illinois, since 1907 when he was a child. First the Whitesides tented and then later stayed in the upstairs rooms of the Inn. They knew the Gregorys in Chicago through Nathaniel Sr.'s brother, William.

Inez (Arnold, Gould) Rea began coming to Gregory's in 1932 after her husband died. It did not take her long to choose a lot up the hill behind the Inn and the two cow pastures. She designed the cottage to wrap around huge existing trees and hired Frank Petrosky to build it. Completed in 1933, the exterior and the interior staircase are constructed of redwood. Most of the interior is pine, including the wide planked porch floor which shows a lot of wear. This porch still has some of the original screening. The French doors came from Hinsdale, Illinois, along with the sofa and platform chairs.

The cottage remains essentially as it was built with exposed studs. The large living/dining room has a brick fireplace. Bookcases recessed between the studs are filled with books Mrs. Rea brought with her from the small

private rental library she ran in Hinsdale. The cottage is filled with memorabilia such as grandmother's sewing baskets, driftwood and sailing trophies won on Glen Lake by grandchildren, Nathaniel and Barbara Whiteside. They recall sleeping in front of the fireplace when it was cold. The kitchen with its original porcelain sink and drain board once had a woodburning cook stove in the corner which heated water pumped up the hill from Gregory's. A small room for Daisy, the maid, was off the kitchen and was later turned into a dressing room which housed the crib and later a double bed for married grandchildren. For years the only bathroom was across from the dining room table.

The upstairs ceiling-high bedroom walls are natural colored Celotex with exposed ceiling rafters above. Barbara remembers sleeping in the north bedroom, formerly her grandmother's and later her son William's. It still has the hole in the wall that her brother Nathaniel drilled to spy on her. They both loved spending the entire summer with their grandmother, from the day school got out until the day they returned to Hinsdale. Their father would come up on weekends.

Mrs. Rea planted pine trees and lilacs which have grown and now obscure their once magnificent view of the entire Glen Lake. She loved gardening, had a rock terraced wildflower garden and put in her own well to water her garden. She also loved socializing with her friends, Mrs. Barton and Mrs. Dickinson. As was the custom of the day, she kept a guest book where she also recorded teas held for twelve people from the local summer colony. She also listed expenses and cottage linens. Barbara recalls that Mrs. Gregory encouraged cottage owners on the hill to dine at her resort and to use the music room, library and dock as long as they obeyed the quiet time during Mrs. Gregory's afternoon nap.

Six generations of the family have been coming to Glen Lake, and Barbara believes it was a good way to grow up: learning to respect their elders while knowing they were your good friends. It was a quiet and peaceful, good life. Children knew and played with neighboring children and were always content and busy, often inventing their own fun. She fondly refers to this cottage as "an ancient funny place with wild things in it" and to Glen Lake as her "home." After Mrs. Rea's death in 1945, the cottage remained in the family with its integrity intact.

1933

INEZ REA • NATHANIEL AND MILDRED WHITESIDE COTTAGE

BUILDER: Frank Petrosky, Glen Arbor, Michigan

COTTAGE: Two-story lap-sided un-winterized cottage with open stud construction

INTERIOR: Living room/dining room with pine beaded board, redwood staircase and brick fireplace, kitchen, four bedrooms and maid's room, front screened porch with attached garage underneath

LANDSCAPE FEATURE: Curved entrance stairway and retainer wall, stone barbeque

LOT: 100 by 400 feet with 50-foot shared dock and lake access easement

MAP LOCATION: F6, #157

CASPARIS LOG COTTAGE

Dr. Horton R. and Frances (Kelley) Casparis of Nashville, Tennessee, first came to Glen Lake in the 1920s. For several seasons they stayed in the Robinson and Goodell cottages on the east shore. They often played golf at the Glen Lake Country Club which was located on the hill behind the cottages. Dr. and Mrs. Casparis fell in love with Glen Lake. They purchased some land and drew up their plans.

In 1935 they engaged Joe Gersh of Cedar, Michigan, to build a log cottage and other outbuildings. It was built with tamarack logs that had seasoned in a swamp. The cottage consisted of a vaulted ceiling living/dining room that included a fieldstone fireplace and a built-in bunkbed, a kitchen, two bedrooms and a front porch that ran the length of the cottage. The bunkbed became a staging area for plays performed by the children through several generations. As the cottage was built before indoor plumbing, showers, or hot water, the family and their guests and neighbors went down to the lake with bars of soap to take their baths every afternoon around 4 p.m.

A flat-roofed boathouse on the shoreline provided favorite seating for watching weather changes and sunsets over Alligator Hill. The two small cottages, one for guests and one for servants, were built in the area behind the cottage, along with an outhouse. The guest cottage had an attached carport and the servant's cottage was not much larger than the size of a double bed. The outhouse eventually boasted a flush toilet.

Dr. Casparis was a pediatrician from Texas and Mrs. Casparis a registered nurse. They met while in training at Johns Hopkins Hospital. Mrs. Casparis, from a small Kentucky farm community, chose Johns Hopkins after seeing the school advertised on a thermometer. The Casparises' had two children, Anthony Drake nicknamed Tony and Margaret nicknamed Peggy, who was born just after the cabin was completed.

Following her husband's untimely death in 1942, Mrs. Casparis made a commitment to keep the cottage and make the two-day road trip almost every summer. One summer the family station wagon, clocking about 35 miles per hour, transported grandmother, mother, aunt, Tony with his pet groundhog named Butch, and their dog. Rationing during World War II made food scarce at the lake, and the grown-ups would

(from left) Casparis family, Picnic at North Bar Lake
(Casparis Family Collection)

chase down the delivery trucks to buy bread and milk. Fresh fish, live chickens and homegrown vegetables were found locally. Food was kept cooled in the ice box with ice cut from the lake in winter and kept cold in ice houses insulated with sawdust.

Family fun included climbing the dune or picnicking all day at North Bar Lake in Empire. The wooden picnic basket was packed with plastic plates, cups and utensils, hamburgers and hot dogs. An iron skillet was also brought along with sticks, wood and paper. They built the fire in a hole in the sand and kept their drinks cool in Lake Michigan. Every care in the world went away as they spent day after day swimming and playing at the lakeshore.

Glen Lake has been and continues to be very important in this family's lives, which now includes a fourth generation. Just after Christmas they begin dreaming of the lake and making plans for their summer return. Relatives and friends join in the annual sojourn. The cottage remains in the family, essentially as it was built 70 years ago, with Gersh built log beds, and a log porch table and benches that seat twelve gracing the screened-in porch. Beginning in 1936, the guest books attest to the pleasure and enjoyment of the cottage's hospitality and the beauty of Glen Lake.

1935

HORTON AND FRANCES CASPARIS LOG CABIN

BUILDER: Joe Gersh, Cedar, Michigan

COTTAGE: One-story tamarack log cabin with fieldstone chimney

INTERIOR: Living/dining room with vaulted ceiling, fieldstone fireplace, built-in bed, kitchen, two bedrooms and screened porch across the front

OUTBUILDINGS: Guest house, hired help's cottage, boathouse, outhouse with chemical toilet

FRONTAGE: 60 feet

MAP LOCATION: L8, not numbered

WELLS COTTAGE *(The Bracken)*

Clifford P. "Tubby" and Nell Wells lived in Detroit where he was in charge of overhead lines for Detroit Edison. They began coming to Glen Lake in the 1920s in a Model T and stayed in Dr. Lawrence Day's bunkhouse near Krull's Resort. They purchased a lot on Fisher Point in 1934. In 1936 they built a one-story three-bedroom cottage with a lakeside porch and a separate garage. Their children were Carol (Dexter Wright), C.P., Jr. "Bud" (Mary Redden), and MaryAnne "Twink" (Ralph Forseyth). Friends from Detroit (Ned and Lois Chapman and Roy and Cat Burgess) built cottages on adjacent lots and the three families spent glorious summers together. The grandchildren cherish the family traditions and memories and came up with more than could be included. Days began at 7 a.m. with Tubby's breakfasts of shredded wheat, milk and coffee, raising the flag, recording the daily water temperature and barometer readings. If the temperature was above 55 degrees and not raining, Tubby would prod all house guests to join him for a dip in the lake. Up to seventeen children on the Point played long and hard (catching crayfish, fishing, hunting turtles and snakes, swimming, canoeing, sailing with Uncle Tubby, eating Nana's cookies, playing shuffleboard, taking walks with Nana to see the lady slipper flowers, water skiing with Aunt Betty, watching stars on the dock and then sleeping on the porch.) Cocktails were served on the porch between 5 and 6 pm. Sometimes cocktails lasted longer and the kids were invited to join while Tubby played the piano or accordion for sing-a-longs, often with Lois Chapman who was a professional singer. Family dinners were followed by fun competitive card playing. The looser had to venture with a candle to touch Dr. Hooper's memorial stone, walk up the spooky drive to Bob Byerley's cottage, touch it and sing a crazy song, or row across the channel to the snake pit that later became Tamarack Cove. Visitors' arrivals and departures were announced by ringing the dinner bell. A final wave and ring were given when they could be seen driving on the road across the cove.

The cottage remained in the family until 1990. Dan and Magee Gordon of Grand Rapids purchased it. The Gordons grew up as lake summer residents. Magee's family summered at Mullet Lake, Michigan, when she was young. She met Dan one summer when both were at their family's summer cottages on Gull Lake, Michigan. Dan's family goes back several generations at the Gull Lake Bible Conference. Jack and Kathy Phillips, friends from Gordon Food Service, introduced them to Glen Lake and their family cottage in 1980 when both families had one year-old children. They found themselves being drawn back to Glen Lake and began taking annual two-week vacations with their children Molly, Katybeth and Tommy. They rented for ten years at various cottages around the lake including Peppler's *Birchdale*. While biking, Magee happened upon a for-sale-by-owner sign and they made an appointment to see the cottage. They fell in love with its cozy charm and placed down earnest money. Magee began a correspondence with Carol Wells (Wright) and learned that the cottage had

been named after the bracken fern that covered the point. This pleased the Gordons as bracken plays a large part in their family's favorite books, *The Chronicles of Narnia* by C. S. Lewis.

After seven years the Gordons were able to spend more time at the lake and wanted more comfortable space for family and friends. Their original intent was to put on an addition that would maintain the integrity of the cottage and the connection they felt to the presence of the Wells family. After consulting Mike Collings of Mac Custom Homes, they were disappointed that he recommended taking it down. The old cottage had foundation problems and needed more than a face-lift. He was willing, however, to help them duplicate the original cottage details they wanted retained. They took careful photographs and he meticulously replicated the rooms utilizing the same design elements. The one-car garage was retained.

The screened porch was duplicated, as were the beamed living/dining room ceiling, corner bedroom vanities, bookshelves above the windows, door-less closets, and curved shower enclosure. They reused knotty-pine tongue-and-groove walls both from the original cottage and from one at Gull Lake. A fieldstone fireplace with small stones was built with a new mantel carved with the Sleeping Bear and her cubs. The new shower arch incorporated a lamp post from the now torn down Midland Hotel at Gull Lake. The Wellses' fireplace mantel was placed in the master bedroom. Magee incorporated additional design elements of Adirondack and Muskoka area cottages. The new roof line enhanced the simple charm of the original cottage.

Once the cottage was finished, Tubby's piano, a bookcase filled with old books, porch rattan table and chairs were returned to the cottage and have melded with Gordon family antiques and memories. Tubby's granddaughter, Sue Danielson, still summers a few doors away. Now when she visits the cottage, she feels as if she is still walking into her Nana's cottage, a sign of a successful clone. Meanwhile, the Gordons have established their own family traditions, singing around the campfire, hanging out on the porch and racing to see who is first off the dock. This cottage is a tribute to a successful effort that retains the essence of cottage life.

1936

CLIFFORD AND NELL WELLS COTTAGE
(The Bracken)

COTTAGE: One-story wood frame with wide lap-siding

INTERIOR: Living/dining room with brick fireplace, kitchen and three bedrooms

1997 REBUILD: Two-story wood frame with wide lap-siding, living/dining room with fieldstone fireplace, kitchen, office, two bedrooms, laundry room on first floor, two bedrooms and sitting/game room upstairs

BUILDER: Mike Collings of Mac Custom Homes

OUTBUILDING: Original one-car garage

LANDSCAPE FEATURES: Shuffleboard, fieldstone grill, birch log bonfire pit, split rail fence and stone lamp entrance posts

FRONTAGE: 145 feet

MAP LOCATION: J4, #118

FISHER • HOUSE COTTAGE *(Scotch Pine)*

Eugene "Gene" Fisher was the son of Frank Fisher and grandson of Glen Arbor pioneer John Fisher. He was D.H. Day's driver before he began chauffeuring summer resorters around the lake and picking them up at the dock and train in Traverse City. In 1937 he purchased this property from Nan Helm and built a home and four cottages on the southeast shore of Glen Lake in Burdickville. Being a millwright by trade, he was talented with his hands and machinery. He built a gas-powered boat, *Miss Leelanau*, and operated a pleasure and trout fishing excursions for hire business from the dock at his home.

In about 1943, Gene sold the property to Tom and Eileen (Charter) House who named the resort, Maplecroft. They built a fifth cottage, *Sweet Briar*, and named the others *Cedar Grove, Maplecroft, Pine Knot* and *Scotch Pine*. House was Scottish and had served in the British Navy. He was well-known around the lake and loved every aspect of sailing. He sold Wood Pussey sailboats and rented them for $25 a week, but only after one had taken his lessons. Their two children, Janet and Garth, were sailors. House ran a sailing camp with a fleet of nearly a dozen eight-foot dinghies he had built. When he launched a new boat he played the bagpipes. In 1976 House moved to the Charters' home in Burdickville.

George and Jane (Clark) Van Vleck were from Hinsdale, Illinois. Jane had been coming to Glen Lake since a child, staying in a Tonawathya cottage. When House divided the property in 1971, they purchased the north half with three cottages. In the spring of 1976 they bought the second half with the house and two cottages. That summer George passed away and Jane moved up here to run the Van Vleck Cottages. Five years later she sold the property to the north. Their home and two cottages remain in the family. The cozy charm of this small cottage has been retained.

1937

EUGENE AND LILLIAN FISHER •
TOM AND EILEEN HOUSE *(Scotch Pine)*

BUILDER: Clarence Savage, Glen Arbor

COTTAGES: Wood frame construction clad with lap-siding

INTERIOR: Living/dining/kitchen, fieldstone fireplace, two bedrooms

FRONTAGE: 100 feet

MAP LOCATION: K10, not numbered

Gene Fisher, chauffeur   *(Whiteside Family Collection)*

Miss Leelanau   *(Conroy Family Collection)*

SPOUSE COTTAGE

In 1933 Charles, a dental supply salesman, and his wife Mildred (Baetschi, Vogel) Spouse from Toledo, Ohio, began renting on Little Glen. Her previous husband, Charles Vogel, had been a civil engineer who had died as a result of pneumonia contracted while working on Toledo's sewers. Between 1935 and 1938 their three teenage sons, Charles Wesley, Jr., George A. (Barbara Coppens) and Dr. Richard Keith (Marit Dorsey) Vogel, tented on this property which had an outhouse and a well. They had to first clear the area of the trash they had left on the property while renting next-door at the cottage owned by the Hodges, who were relatives of the Dorseys. Their parents continued to rent from the Hodges, and the boys sometimes drove themselves in their 1936 secondhand Plymouth. While up here, Richard drove a dune buggy for the Warneses in Glen Haven.

Built in 1938 on the south shore of Little Glen on Welch Road, this cottage began as a single room bunkhouse built of wide Ponderosa pine boards with cross beams and a high ceiling. A few years later a summer kitchen, running water and electricity were added. In 1947, a two-story addition was built for Spouse's retirement. A Native American stonemason from Lake Leelanau, particular about wanting wet Lake Michigan stones as they split better, built the cut-fieldstone wall in the game room. The stones were gathered south of Empire and delivered by Matt Breithaupt and his team of horses.

In 1968 Mildred Spouse sold the cottage to the second owners, Norbert and Joanne Sprouse of Columbus, Indiana. The Sprouses and their two sons, Stephen and Bradford, used it as a summer cottage until Joanne moved to Glen Lake permanently in 1988. The kitchen contains a butcher's block purchased from Deering's Market in Empire and a small wood heat stove added in the late 1970s. This cottage is an excellent example of how the original cottage charm and integrity can be maintained through additions and renovations.

1938

CHARLES AND MILDRED SPOUSE COTTAGE

Builder: Joe Dhuyvetter, Empire, Michigan
(Joan Harriger's father)

COTTAGE: One-room wood frame bunkhouse with vertical
wood siding, corner windows and a large window facing the lake

INTERIOR: One large room with wood cross beams, high ceiling
and Ponderosa pine board walls, fireplace, and wood floors

1940-1941 ADDITION: Running water and electricity installed,
summer kitchen with wood cookstove and screened porch built
on the southeast end of bunkhouse

1947 ADDITION: Two-story addition built by Lloyd Gibson of
Leland on the west side added three-paned casement windows;
entry/game room with cut-stone wall, two downstairs bedrooms,
laundry room, one upstairs bedroom with walk-in attic above the
two lower bedrooms, a Michigan cellar, a boiler and a pressure
tank; bookcases built on either side of the cut-stone fireplace in
the living room (original bunkhouse)

2000 RENOVATION: Kitchen and replacement of windows

OUTBUILDINGS: Two-car garage built 1940-1941, potting
shed earlier housed the outhouse

LANDSCAPE FEATURE: Stone wall along circular driveway

FRONTAGE: 188 feet (three grandfathered lots)

MAP LOCATION: C8, not numbered

DICKINSON COTTAGE

Fred and Julia Dickinson with
Terry on her lap, Grace and
William
(*Dickinson Family Collection*)

Frederick William Dickinson began coming to Glen Lake from Chicago in 1912 with his parents, William Frederick and Ruth Dickinson, and grandparents, Joseph and Elizabeth Bray. They first stayed at King's Resort on Little Glen and later Gregory's. His grandparents built Bray Cottage on the south shore of Little Glen Lake in 1914 and then his parents built their cottage next door in 1923. Both cottages are across the road from this cottage.

Fred lived his childhood years in Oak Park, Illinois, until his father, an attorney, became Vice-President of Rock Island Railroad and moved to Hinsdale which was located on the railroad. When Fred was five years old, he first arrived in Glen Haven by ship and spotted a man photographing the gala arrival. This began a lifelong fascination with cameras that Fred pursued full time when he moved, as a single man, to this cottage located across the road from his parents' cottage. He and his mother designed

it and John Hatlem built it in 1938. The two-story cottage has interior upstairs bedroom windows that provide light and air circulation to the two-story living room and parlor below. He also purchased forty acres to the west from the Dorseys and ten acres to the east formerly owned by the Tobins. As a child, Fred had assisted in the construction of his parents' fieldstone boathouse by wetting the stones prior to their being set in mortar. Through the years, using a trailer he pulled behind his car, he enjoyed gathering stones from farmers' fields. He used these stones to build retaining walls and define his garden.

Julia Terry's family summered on Lake Leelanau at their cottage, *Gracewood*. She worked as a librarian for three years at Finch Junior College in New York City but wanted to move to this area to be closer to her summer home. In 1938 Julia began writing a weekly column for the *Leelanau Enterprise*. In 1941 she took a job working for the newspa-

per in Leland which paid $10 a week, furnished her a car, and allowed her to live on the second floor of the building. Fred had heard there was new good-looking redhead working there, so he took in a map he knew they would not be able to print, just to get to meet her. They were married six weeks later. They bought the *Leelanau Enterprise* in May 1943, and Julia became the editor and a mother at the same time as their first child, Grace Esther, was born. Tired of the commute, they built a studio building next to their home on Glen Lake and ran the presses and office from there. They had two more children, William Frederick and Terry Dyer. They sold the newspaper in 1948, at which time it moved back to Leland. The old lithograph press was given to the Leelanau Historical Museum. Fred then opened his photography gallery, The Studio.

Julia continued to work while raising her children. She also continued her weekly column in the *Enterprise* until 1999. In 1951, she wrote *The Story of Leelanau* and, in 1993, transcribed and edited *The Boizard Letters* from her office, the children's old playroom. She taught school in Empire, Leland, and Glen Lake. Julia was Leelanau School's librarian and later set up the library at the newly established Interlochen Art Academy. She was known for the faculty Christmas parties and Glen Lake Woman's Club meetings she held in their home which had great entertainment space.

Fred and Julia befriended many and were loved and respected in the community. With his friend Arthur S. Huey, Fred established the Prospectors Club and together they wrote the by-laws by hand in Fred's living room. Fred was from a family that had several artists, and he devoted his life to documenting the beauty of the area through photography and map drawing. This tradition has been passed down to his daughter, Grace, who continues the production and hand-coloring of the photographs from his original negatives in The Studio. Later in life Fred began oil painting and many of his paintings continue to hang in their home. He died in 2000. The home retains its original integrity, art and furniture.

1938

FREDERICK AND JULIA DICKINSON COTTAGE

BUILDER: John Hatlem, Burdickville, Michigan

COTTAGE: Two-story wood frame structure clad with wide lap-siding originally painted white with green trim

INTERIOR: Cedar walls and Douglas-fir floors, first floor living room (later playroom and office) dining room, and kitchen, one large upstairs room

EARLY 1940S ADDITION: Fourteen foot high gabled ceiling living room with cut granite fireplace and chimney built by Sharnowski brothers, Cedar, Michigan

1951 REMODELING: Upstairs room converted into three bedrooms with painted Celotex walls, tongue-and-groove doors made by Hatlem, metal grates installed in the interior windows which looked down into the second living room converted into children's playroom, glass block interior window

OUTBUILDINGS: One-story four-room photography studio building with poured 12" concrete walls built mid 1940s to house the *Leelanau Enterprise* presses and office, later became The Studio; one-car garage with poured concrete floor and foundation that is three feet high in back due to being built into the hill, 12' x 12' foot pitch roof allows second-story storage; precut wood kit garage with Dutch-lap siding located originally just off the road so as to minimize winter plowing later moved to the south of The Studio

MAP LOCATION: D9, not numbered

Dean Cottage

Samuel E. and Lillian (Hope) Dean of Hinsdale, Illinois, were introduced to Glen Lake by bridge playing friends Wade and Margaret Fetzer. The Dean children were Helen (Harold Grumhaus), Samuel E. Jr. (Dorothy), Howard (Elizabeth), Stuart (Cora), and Patricia (John Rockwood). Even though the children were nearly raised, Dean liked the idea of buying a summer place in his home state of Michigan. He was then president of Dean Evaporated Milk which had introduced paper milk cartons to the industry. Their architect Harford Field had built their son Samuel's home in Oak Brook, Illinois. Not having visited this site, Field couldn't have known the contours of the land and the need for the garage to be built under the cottage. It was completed in 1938 after at least a year of building by Joe Gersh.

This grand cottage has a central two-story living room with cedar rafters and a cut-fieldstone fireplace showcasing Samuel Jr.'s moose trophy. A lakeside porch runs the width of the living room. The dining room table with its log base and some of the porch furniture are original as well as two double log bunkbeds built by Joe Gersh. The family's help, a couple, lived above the kitchen. The cottage remains in the family and has kept its integrity.

A horse stable with a mud floor was built on the property at the same time as the cottage. Patricia, their youngest daughter, brought her horse Jepp up for the summer. She had just completed her senior year of high school and would ride her horse alone on Miller Hill which was some distance from their cottage. She met her future husband, John Rockwood, that first summer on the beach in front of their cottages. The stable was moved up near the house in the late 1940s or early 1950s and became a guest house.

Mrs. Lillian Dean with Jepp, 1937   (*Rockwood Family Collection*)

Samuel E. Dean, Sr. sitting on the dock, 1937   (*Rockwood Family Collection*)

Dining Room, 1937

(Rockwood Family Collection)

1938

SAMUEL AND LILLIAN DEAN COTTAGE

ARCHITECT: Harford Field, Hinsdale, Illinois

BUILDER: Joe Gersh, Cedar, Michigan

COTTAGE: Two-story wood frame clad in cedar shakes with divided-light casement windows

INTERIOR: Living room, dining room, kitchen, front porch, five bedrooms and three bathrooms

2001–2 RENOVATION: Extended kitchen end, added second stairwell leading to master bedroom suite, replaced major windows

OUTBUILDING: Stable now a guest cottage

FRONTAGE: 250 feet

MAP LOCATION: H4, not numbered

WEESE COTTAGES

Harry E. Weese first came to the area to fish with Indiana relatives and friends in 1921. Weese, who worked for Harris Trust and Savings Bank in downtown Chicago, Illinois, lived in Kenilworth. They had a summer cottage in Barrington so that his family could experience rural life. Taken with the beauty of Glen Lake, he and his wife Marjorie L.S. (Mohr) vacationed with their five children Harry, Jane, John, Sue and Ben. They stayed at Ocker's Resort, Bloom Cottages and the Vlack cottages. In 1925 Weese purchased 1000 feet, ten lakeshore lots, on the southwest side of Glen Lake from Indiana friends who had taken his recommendation to come to Glen Lake and start a summer colony. He kept four lots for his family and sold the others to Hagerty (2), Dralla (2), Drake, and Hamilton.

Ten years later during a family dinner discussion, a decision was made to build a log cabin at Glen Lake, rather than buying an Airstream trailer and traveling. The Weeses commissioned their eldest son, Harry Mohr Weese, a young architectural student at MIT, to design the cottage.

For many years, the senior Weese commuted on the weekends by driving to Manitowoc, Wisconsin, to take the overnight ferry to Frankfort, Michigan, where he was met by the family station wagon and driven to the cottage in time for breakfast at 7:30 a.m. He returned by the Sunday night boat to Manitowoc, having had a good night's sleep before driving to downtown Chicago by 10:00 a.m.

The parents' legacy of family closeness and the love of nature and the land continues in this complex of three family cottages that remain virtually unchanged. All designed by Harry, they stand as rare examples of early residential designs by an architect who became recognized nationally and internationally. Brothers John and Ben also became architects. Succeeding generations have produced an impressive number of architects, landscape architects and graphic designers.

Four-year old Harry Mohr Weese grew up and built three sailboats on Glen Lake with the help of his brothers
(Weese Family Collection)

Two-year old Sue Weese on Ocker's dock
(Weese Family Collection)

"Glen Lake was the inspiration for two sailboats built by Harry, the second with John's help, and a third by Ben. In looking back over the various activities designed for the benefit of growing children and to help in their raising, I can easily conclude that the Glen Lake cottage was the best investment the family ever made. There is complete agreement that if we had not discovered this beautiful lake and its surrounding country, we would have missed much of the "joy of living." Vacations continue to be spent there by the various children and the grandchildren, and there is good prospect that *Shack Tamarack* will be their headquarters for summer vacations for years to come."

— Harry E. Weese
From Bull Creek to Barrington, 1952

Shack Tamarack

Even though Harry E. and Marjorie L.S. (Mohr) Weese commissioned their son Harry to design the cottage, the entire family became involved with the design and planning. This grand cottage was constructed of tamarack logs, one measuring sixty feet long. The logs had been cut the previous winter, stripped and stored by Joe and Frank Gersh, builders from Cedar, Michigan.

Construction was completed in six weeks during the summer of 1936. The Gershes also built much of the furniture including a large dining room table made from two 20-inch wide white pine planks with matching benches and double and three-quarter bunk beds. Three of the seven bedrooms are bunkrooms, with separate exterior entrances off a balcony and back exterior stairway. These bunkrooms have high open areas by the ceiling for light and air circulation to the large living area below. The children remember hearing the fire popping, seeing the firelight glow on the ceiling and listening to adult conversation and card playing well into the night.

1936

ARCHITECT: Harry Mohr Weese, Kenilworth, Illinois

BUILDER: Joe and Frank Gersh, Cedar, Michigan

COTTAGE: Two-story round log cottage with notched corners, boulders used for support piers, exterior back stairway to three bunkrooms

INTERIOR: Two-story living area with fieldstone fireplace, dining area, kitchen, seven bedrooms, screened porch, yellow pine floors

OUTBUILDINGS: Log carport

FRONTAGE: 100 feet

MAP LOCATION: G9, not numbered

COTTAGE *Number Two*

Frequent guests to *Shack Tamarack* soon necessitated spillover space. Harry Weese again turned to his son to work on a design for the second cottage they would name *Number Two*.

Built in 1939, the cottage was innovative in design and utilized natural materials and simple balloon frame construction. The cottage is reminiscent of the farmhouses Harry had seen on a 1937 bicycle trip in Sweden. The main room of the cottage has sliding windowed walls that access a terrace. The living room has black cherry vertical lap-siding on one wall and paneling on the other. A freestanding fireplace unit, assisted by insulated walls, heats the cottage. The ceilings are Celotex.

1939

Cottage *Number Two*

Architect: Harry Mohr Weese,
Kenilworth, Illinois

Builder: Joe and Frank Gersh, Cedar, Michigan

Cottage: One-story balloon wood frame construction

Interior: Large living/dining/kitchen area with free
standing fireplace, four bedrooms off a corridor, screened
porch floor had a deck laid on top of the split-fieldstone
terrace

Frontage: 100 feet

Map Location: G9, not numbered

PRITCHARD COTTAGE

A third cottage was built the same summer as Cottage *Number Two*. Richard E. Pritchard, a banking associate of Harry Weese, purchased the property from Weese and retained their son Harry to design a cottage. Pritchard stipulated that it must contain three bedrooms, a bath and be completed in one summer. He also specified that it cost less than two thousand dollars, including the five hundred dollars paid for the lot and all of the furnishings including curtains. He also did not want to see it until it was finished.

The Pritchard Cottage is more experimental than the other two cottages with interesting features added as a result of the architect's experience of living on the lake.

It is constructed with a single skin of two-inch planking for structure and finish. Sliding glass doors along the living area and hall bedroom corridor open onto a screened porch. A space efficient dining table pivots and rests under the kitchen counter. It also features a dramatic one-way sloping roof. The cottage is kept critter free with a folded sheet metal piece at the base of the floor and walls and a guard cap on the chimney of the prefabricated plaster fireplace.

Some thirty years after being built, the Pritchard family cottage returned to Weese family ownership and remains virtually unchanged.

1939

ARCHITECT: Harry Mohr Weese, Kenilworth, Illinois

BUILDER: Joe and Frank Gersh, Cedar, Michigan

DESCRIPTION: One-story wood plank-sided cottage

INTERIOR: Living/dining/kitchen area with free-standing prefabricated plaster fireplace, three bedrooms off a corridor

FRONTAGE: 100 feet

MAP LOCATION: G9, not numbered

GOMMESEN COTTAGE

For many years before building on Glen Lake, Arthur and Alva Marie Evelyn (Nelson) Gommesen had rented cottages in Glen Arbor and stayed at Martha Andresen's Kum-an-Dyne. They purchased land on Fisher point in 1938 for $500 from Juanita Tracy. Tracy's mother, Dr. Clara Hooper from Toledo, Ohio, was a homeopathic doctor who began the Glen Eden Hotel as a health resort in the 1920s. Dr. Hooper's memorial stone can be found along the side of Fisher Point Road, not far from the Gommesen cottage.

Arthur Gommesen was a furniture designer during the heyday of furniture building in Grand Rapids, Michigan, in the early 1900s. He worked for Berkey & Gay and the Waddell Manufacturing Company designing the then popular ornately carved mahogany furniture. His eye and attention to detail influenced the design of the cabin-style cottage, as well as built-ins, woodwork and most furniture. The cottage reveals Arthur's interest in the newly developing Early American design. Every detail from the mailbox to the brown and white painted wide clapboard siding, the gleaming interior woodwork and kitchen cabinets reflects this design aesthetic. All the interior wood surfaces were finished with a variety of glazes and wood stains most of which were created by Gommesen. He also laid the patio, stone pathway and built an outdoor fieldstone barbecue fireplace.

The Gommesens had two daughters, Marian L. (W. Calvin Patterson) and Esther A. (John B. Kelly). Although too young to compete, Marian applied for the Miss Michigan contest lying about her age. She was chosen Miss Michigan in 1932 and her trophy, a new car, sat in the garage undriven as she was too young to drive and her father was furious with her. Purportedly she never dated the Lott boys at Glen Lake, but at the University of Michigan she dated football center Gerald Ford before he met Betty. A portrait of Marian by the well-known Michigan painter Mathias J. Alten, hangs in the cottage.

Gommesen Guest Cotta

1939

ARTHUR AND ALVA GOMMESEN

BUILDER: Joe Gersh, Cedar, Michigan

COTTAGE: One-story wood frame cottage clad with painted wide lap-siding and window shutters with shutter dogs

INTERIOR: Living room with cut fieldstone fireplace, dining room, kitchen, drop-shuttered porch, two bedrooms

OUTBUILDINGS: One-room guesthouse with cut and full fieldstone chimney built in 1948 along with attached garage and workshop.

LANDSCAPE FEATURES: Fieldstone barbeque fireplace, stone pathways and patio

FRONTAGE: 110 feet

MAP LOCATION: J4, #120

Alva, Arthur and daughter Esther Anne "Trann" taken at their cottage by an iterant photographer

(Gommesen Family Collection)

They made the cottage their year-round residence after his retirement in 1965. Gommesen enjoyed making furniture for himself and his neighbors in his garage workshop and loved painting. One of his paintings rests in tribute on an easel on the enclosed porch. Gommesen designed the 1954 Glen Lake Association map with the wildflower border and cottage owners' names and locations. The previously unpublished map used in this book is also Gommesen's, drawn about the time he built this cottage. The cottage remains in the family virtually unchanged.

HARRIS LOG COTTAGE

The Harris cottage is located in Forest Down, an unrecorded ten-lot subdivision surveyed in 1924 on the southeast side of Glen Lake near Burdickville on Dunn's Farm Road. The subdivision property, with over 1000 feet of lake frontage, was originally owned by D.H. Day who used the land for his logging operations. Forest Downs preceded Day's larger 1927 Day Forest Estate Development on Alligator Hill and Day's death in 1928.

D.H. Day owned Glen Haven and the sawmill at the east end of Little Glen and conducted huge logging operations on land surrounding Glen Lake. They cut logs in the hills and skidded them down to the shore in the winter. They were then stacked and chained together and towed by tug or barge in log booms to the mill in spring. A logging road paralleled the lake through this subdivision. On Forest Down Lot #1 was the line shack which Day gave as a wedding present to his son D.H., Jr. and wife Helen. The Day family used it as their Glen Lake cottage for years.

Verne L. Harris was a lawyer from Cleveland, Ohio, where he owned real estate, several cemeteries and at least one radio station. In 1937 he was fishing at Glen Lake and discovered that lots were for sale through B.R. Hendel, the representative of sales for D.H. Day's estate. He called his friend Paul O. Flemming, a Cleveland photographer, and they went into partnership to purchase the lots and acreage across Dunn's Farm Road in Burdickville. After agreeing that log cottages be built on the lots, they began selling them for $15 a front foot.

They began construction on their own cottages about the same time. Harris' was smaller, measuring 24' x 28', and was completed first in 1939. Paul and Dorothy Flemming built a two-bedroom next door and named it *Flamingo Cottage* after his studio name. There eventually were five adjacent log cottages all built by Joe Gersh. The furthest south was moved to Bow Road when a new home was built in the 1990s.

Verne and Dorothy Harris summered in their cottage with their only child Carol (Hoyt) who inherited it. She sold it in 1993 to Betty Rhoades whose only change was to add a loft.

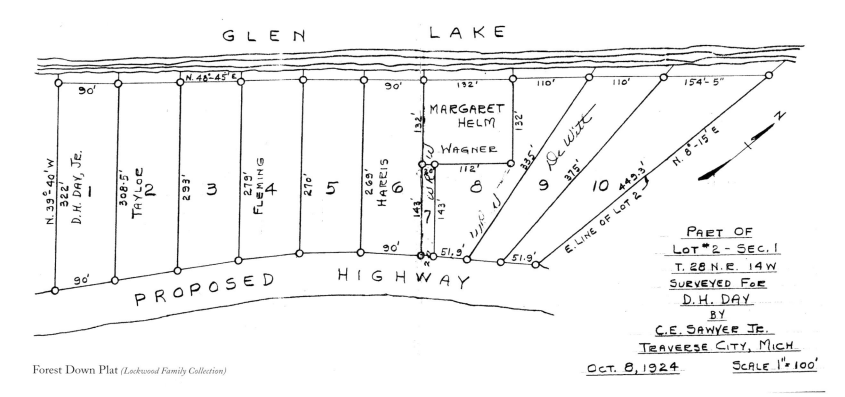

GLEN LAKE

PROPOSED HIGHWAY

N. 48°-45' E

N. 39°-40' W

90'

322'
D.H. DAY, JR.
1

90'

308.5'
TAYLOR
2

293'
3

279'
FLEMING
4

270'
5

269'
HARRIS
6

90'

143'

7

143'

51.9'

MARGARET
HELM

WAGNER

132'

132'

112'

8

132'

335'

DE WITT
9

375'

110'

10

449.3'
E. LINE OF LOT 2

110'

154'-5"

N. 8°-15' E

N

51.9'

PART OF
LOT #2 - SEC. 1
T. 28 N.R. 14 W
SURVEYED FOR
D. H. DAY
BY
C.E. SAWYER JR.
TRAVERSE CITY, MICH
OCT. 8, 1924   SCALE 1"=100'

Forest Down Plat *(Lockwood Family Collection)*

Paul and Dorothy Flemming in *Flamingo Cottage*   *(Vintage Views Archives)*

1939

**VERNE AND DOROTHY HARRIS
LOG COTTAGE**

BUILDER: Joe Gersh and Frank
Peplinski, Cedar, Michigan

COTTAGE: One-story full-round
cedar log cabin with notched joints,
cut and whole fieldstone chimney

INTERIOR: Living/dining room,
kitchen, bedroom and front porch

FRONTAGE: 90 feet

MAP LOCATION: K9; not numbered

ROHR • ZELLE COTTAGE

In 1925 Jerome Stock purchased 1000 feet on the northern "Gold Coast" shore of Glen Lake and divided it into 100-foot lots. He sold this lot to Winfield and Ethel Rohr of Toledo, Ohio, in 1937. Mr. Rohr was connected to Proctor and Gamble. As they did not have children, the property was sold after Mrs. Rohr's death in 1961.

The cottage was built in 1939 by Frank Petroskey of Lake Leelanau. He also built similar cottages for Roy and Mabel Deng of Hinsdale, Illinois, to the east and for the Cohens to the west. These were classic cedar cottages with 15-foot lakestone fireplaces, cathedral ceilings in the central room and a loft bedroom.

Dr. Kane and Libby Zelle of Springfield, Illinois, purchased the cottage in the summer of 1961 when they were visiting friends, Bob and Helen Patton. As the story goes, Doctors Zelle and Patton walked down the beach one dark night and peered in the windows. Dr. Zelle bought the cottage without ever going inside and without consulting his wife. The cottage came furnished including a large

supply of boxed Swan Soap flakes and bars of Fels Naptha soap, used to wash off poison ivy oils. The Rohrs' presence was felt by the Zelles whenever they looked at the large print of moose hunters, a painting of cows or Mrs. Rohr's sewing basket. The Zelles added a second bathroom with a porthole window salvaged from the *Francisco Morazon*, the steamer wrecked off the shoals of South Manitou Island in 1960. The living room table also was made from *Morazon* hatch covers.

The Zelles also added baseboard heat and came up for Christmas in 1962. Chick Lanphier gave snowmobile rides and Tom Dean took them through the deep snow to cut their Christmas tree. Looking forward to baked beans cooked in an iron pot hanging over the fireplace fire, the family, however, was hit by the flu. One by one they fell ill, until the only person left standing was Susan, aged 8, who got sick first and recovered in time to take care of the rest. Needless to say, no one ate the beans.

The garage provided a workshop space for Dr. Zelle where he posted this sign: "Avenge yourself! Live long enough to be a problem to your children." Dr. Zelle named the cottage *Nepenthe*, the place where he and the family could escape from all cares. For several years they did not have a telephone and used the Pattons' or Lanphiers' party line in case of emergency. *Nepenthe* has changed little and remains a cozy Michigan cedar cottage now belonging to the four Zelle children, Lee, Ann, Carolyn, and Susan.

1939

**WINFIELD AND ESTHER ROHR •
KANE AND LIBBY ZELLE COTTAGE**

BUILDER: Frank Petroskey,
Lake Leelanau, Michigan

COTTAGE: One-story wood construction
clad in stained cedar lap-siding

INTERIOR: Tongue-and-groove cedar
living room with cathedral ceiling,
lakestone fireplace and enclosed loft
bedroom, kitchen, entry room with
beveled cedar, two bedrooms, cellar

1960 ADDITION: Living room skylights
and bookcases, second bathroom, closets,
baseboard heating, deck off porch,
cement patio by the beach

OUTBUILDINGS: Garage with workshop,
laundry room, fishing and skiing storage

FRONTAGE: 100 feet

MAP LOCATION: I4, not numbered

LEWIS LOG COTTAGE

In September 1940, Joseph and Amanda Vlack of Maple City, Michigan, sold property on the east shore of Fisher Lake to William Milton and Dora Elsa Lewis of Cincinnati, Ohio. They had been vacationing on Fisher Lake for years, perhaps at Kingfisher Camp, in log cabins to the north of this property with the Drotts who were also from Cincinnati. The Lewises had seven children and likely built the original two log cottages on the property. The notched corner, full-log cottage appears to be the older and is the one photographed for this book.

Two of the Lewises' daughters and their husbands, Richard and Mildred Siebenthaler and Robert and Ruth Sebastiani, purchased the cottages from their mother in 1974. After some time there was a change in the family relationship and the sisters agreed to sell in 1994 to Andra Pierre and Olivia (Johnson) DuPont from Midland, Michigan. The DuPonts moved this two-bedroom full log cottage further south on the property to make room for a new home. They have renovated the cottages to retain their original integrity. The DuPonts maintain the two log cottages as their guest cottages.

EARLY 1940S

WILLIAM AND DORA LEWIS LOG COTTAGE

COTTAGE: Cedar notched full-log cottage

INTERIOR: Two bedroom cottage with living room and kitchen

EARLY ADDITION: Front screened porch, back enclosed porch and bathroom

SECOND COTTAGE: Three bedroom half-log cottage with similar layout

FRONTAGE: 200 feet

MAP LOCATION: J3, not numbered

Haggarty Cottage

George and Mary (Kirk) Haggarty asked their business friend, George A. Schilling to build them a cottage on 300 of the 1300 foot of property on the east shore of Glen Lake that Schilling had purchased in 1940 from D.H. Day's estate. Schilling chose a design similar to the cottage he had built in 1928 several lots north. Schilling had befriended Joe Gersh while building that cottage and they worked together on the design for this cottage with Gersh drawing it in pencil on a construction board.

Haggarty was a prominent Detroit attorney and entrepreneur who owned radio and TV stations and a race track. He was an athlete who had played basketball and baseball at the University of Michigan and also played golf. The two Georges became close friends as did their wives and their children called the adults aunt and uncle. Each family had three children: Haggartys had Ann (Warren), Martha (Petrie, Bolognini) and George; Schillings had George T. (Barbara White), Dr. Richard (Betty Fink,

Barbara Whiteside) and Nancy (Cheney, Johnson). Sharing a four-party telephone line, each George could hear the other's ring and listen in so as to keep up on Detroit dealings, that is until the other would say, "George, hang up." Schilling was a fisherman and Haggarty, who owned a Chris-Craft, was known to circle round the Shilling's fishing boat in the evening inquiring how the fishing was.

Glen Lake was considered paradise and the Haggartys' time here was cherished and full of memories. A brook running between the cottage and the road made the ground very wet and necessitated a bridge. When it was quiet at night, Ann remembers listening to the trickling water. After Mary died, George retained ownership and brought his second wife here until 1971 when he sold the cottage to Richard Schilling. The cottage is owned by the O'Neill family. The parents started the Woodcock restaurant in Burdickville

1940

GEORGE AND MARY HAGGARTY COTTAGE

BUILDERS: Joe Gersh, Cedar, Michigan

COTTAGE: One-story wood frame cottage clad with wide lap-siding which is painted white with green trim, fieldstone chimney

INTERIOR: Knotty pine tongue-and-groove interior walls, Douglas-fir flooring, central living/dining room, cut-fieldstone fireplace, kitchen, four bedrooms, and front porch

LATE 1980s STABILIZATION: Over the years the heavy chimney sank and pulled the floorboards with it; the two were separated, the floor jacked up and a new hearth placed on top of the old to fill the space.

OUTBUILDINGS: Guesthouse and carport no longer exist as new houses have been built on the 100 feet on each side

FRONTAGE: 300 feet, now 100

MAP LOCATION: L7, not numbered

PEPPLER COTTAGE *(Birchdale)*

(Peppler Family Collection)

Henry L. and Iva Myrtle (McHenry) Peppler of Detroit were introduced to Glen Lake in the mid-1920s by his sister Louise and her husband, Christian Krull. The Krulls had just purchased the property where Nessen's Glen Arbor Lumber Company had operated a sawmill on the north shore of Glen Lake at Lake Street. Chris had come up to work in the orchards on Miller Hill. He would sail to and from his work. The Krulls began resort operations out of the main lodge building on Lake Street. Meals were served for guests staying in the upstairs rooms and the lumberjack cottages which had been moved to the beach. Henry Peppler had a two-week vacation from his job as a patternmaker doing castings for Ford Motor Company in Detroit. It took two days to drive their Model T on the dirt roads, staying the night in Cadillac.

In 1939 the Pepplers purchased one of four lots from Dr. Lawrence Day on Northwood Drive. Dr. Day was D. H. Day's nephew from Detroit who also had stayed at Krull's and purchased adjacent property. Day had sold the other lots to Henry's brother Thomas Peppler, Ray Greene, and Col. Thomas Barrett. The Pepplers had Cloys Rader build two rental cottages on the property they named *Birchdale*. The front one was built in 1939; the back cottage was built in 1941 and has the date carved in the fieldstone front wall. As the plans for the cottages were being made, Peppler's son William met Rader's daughter Helen. They were married in 1941, three months before William went overseas for three and one half years in the service.

The cottage is a charmer with original stencils adorning dresser drawers and surrounding the casement windows. The log table and chairs are handmade Habitant furniture from Bay City. The tiny bathroom originally did not have a sink but had a metal shower four steps down to the garage level which was concealed behind a wood closet door that locked from the outside.

1941

HENRY AND IVA PEPPLER COTTAGE *(Birchdale)*

BUILDER: Cloys Rader, Glen Arbor, Michigan

COTTAGE: One-and-one-half-story wood frame cottage clad with painted lap-siding, divided-light wood casement windows

INTERIOR: Cedar interior with log beams, stairwell and balcony, ceiling slopes from two loft bedrooms to a front fieldstone wall with fireplace and firewood cook stove, original linoleum floor in living/dining/kitchen

1960s ADDITION: A front room towards the lake, attached garage converted into bedroom, bath and laundry

FRONT RENTAL COTTAGE: Built in 1939 was incorporated into a year round home around 1984 when William Peppler retired

FRONTAGE: 100 feet

MAP LOCATION: G4, not numbered

(Peppler Family Collection)

Glen Lake Yacht Club

Glen Lake has traditionally been known as a good sailing lake. In the early years of summer residents, open class racing was originally held among several families including the Kilgour, Fetzer, Danly and Wells families. By the late 1930s, Snipe sailboat races were held twice weekly, alternating weeks between Dunn's Farm and Gregory's Tonawathya, along with a yearly regatta. Organizational meetings were held at Jay and Rachel Hench's Tonawathya cottage. It soon became apparent there was a need for a yacht club building for sailing and social events.

In 1939 John Patton, James Johnson and Kay Hench formed a committee to solicit eighteen families to contribute $200 each to become charter members.

A lot with 150 feet of shoreline on Sunset Drive was purchased for $1500. It is on the site of the former D.H. Day Estates Air Field. The clubhouse design submitted by Harford Field, Hinsdale, Illinois, was chosen over Harry Weese's, of Barrington, Illinois. Glen Arbor contractor Frank Petrosky's construction bid of $4100 was accepted. Despite the impending war, construction proceeded and

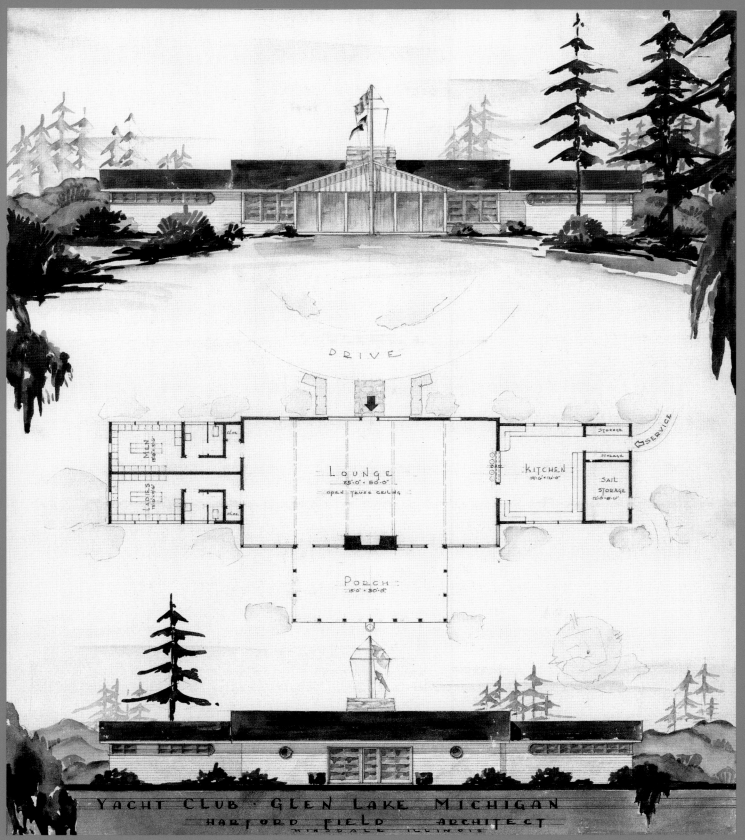

YACHT CLUB · GLEN LAKE MICHIGAN
HARFORD FIELD ARCHITECT
HINSDALE ILLINOIS

1941 Harford Field Glen Yacht Club blueprint and drawing

the club house was completed in time for the 1941 season. After its first successful season, activities waned as the men were at war. The few women who were here summers during the war years faithfully sent newsletters to Yacht Club servicemen and their families. Seventy families gathered at the club and celebrated the day after the war ended on August 14, 1945.

Snipe racing occurred between 1935 and 1955 with as many as twenty-one Snipes racing. Their popularity was enhanced by member Ray Greene who built many of them. He was joined by sailors Hench, Johnson, Fetzer, Hindman, Byerly, Gilroy, Burr, Dean, Weese, Faust, McCally, Miller, White, Schilling, Krull, Deng, Saxon, Williams, Whiteside, Smith and House. Exchange Regattas were held with Leland and Portage Lake. The Glen Lake Snipers traveled throughout Michigan to compete at Traverse City, Diamond Lake, Eagle Lake and Gull Lake, and to Illinois at Crystal Lake and Chicago. The Snipe District Championship was held here in 1961.

1941

GLEN LAKE YACHT CLUB

ARCHITECT: Harford Field, Hinsdale, Illinois

BUILDER: Frank Petrosky

EXTERIOR: Wood frame construction clad with wide lap-siding painted white

INTERIOR: Large main room with cut-stone fireplace and log mantle, kitchen, two locker rooms, storage

EARLY 1950S: Cement front steps with covered roof

MID-1950S REMODELING: Manager's room replaced one locker room and shower was added

1979: Deck enlarged overlooking the lake

FRONTAGE: 150 feet

MAP LOCATION: G5, not numbered

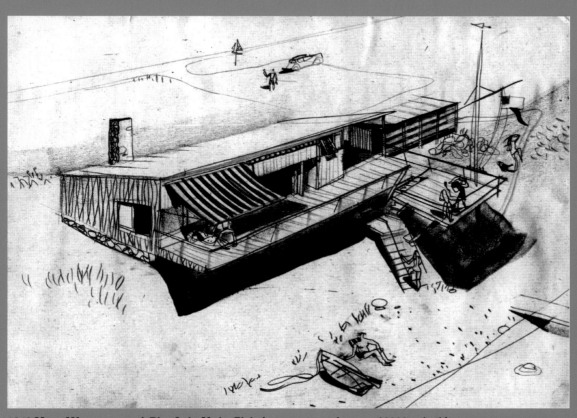

1940 Harry Weese proposed Glen Lake Yacht Club design estimated to cost $3000 to build (*Leelanau Press Collection*)

FIELD COTTAGE *(Hartheoma)*

An architect from Hinsdale, Illinois, Harford Field first came to Glen Lake in 1940, on an invitation to submit a design for the clubhouse of the newly formed Glen Lake Yacht Club. His design was selected and as he and Mary (Hargett) immediately fell in love with the lake, they purchased seven and a half acres for $10 a front foot between the Yacht Club's property and the corner of Sunset and M-22. Field swiftly drew up plans for their home including comprehensive material specifications. Foreseeing the shortage of building supplies caused by the impending war, he stockpiled supplies in a barn owned by his neighbor, Jay Hench, making his last of several deliveries in January 1942. The builder, Frank Petrosky, broke ground in the spring of 1942 with a crew not used to digging basements.

As sand kept caving into the hole dug by a team of horses and a scoop, they had to dig a hole four times the size actually needed and had a huge job backfilling with sand that had fallen down the bluff.

To optimize their view of the lake, Field designed the living room in the front of the house to be an inverted V, with glass on both sides. The 22' x 22' in plan living room, built of tamarack and spruce, was heated by a stone fireplace which handled 42" logs and a heatilator. He surrounded the house with a cedar fence and gate. The Fields had two children, Theola Pearl (Krull) and Harford, Jr. They named their home *Hartheoma* derived from their names and chosen by Mrs. Field as it sounded Indian.

After finishing the house, Field served in the World War II. He moved his family to Glen Lake in 1949 and opened his architectural office in Traverse City, with an expanded design repertoire. In addition to designing several Glen Lake homes and the Glen Lake Yacht Club, he designed Glen Arbor's Christian Scientist Church and several Traverse City churches, a bank, a stadium, and a power plant. They purchased the Woodland Cottages adding several more and rented them out for a number of years.

In 1967 John A. Meaden of Hinsdale purchased the cottage for $50,000 for the fiftieth birthday of his wife Mary (Floyd). They had been vacationing at Glen Lake since the 1950s, staying at the Woodlands, and were friends with Robert and June Nissen. The cottage remains in their family and they have preserved its original essence along with most of the furniture. Son Jay feels that it is a spiritual place.

1942

HARFORD AND MARY FIELD COTTAGE

ARCHITECT: Harford Field

BUILDER: Frank Petrosky

COTTAGE: One-story wood frame construction clad with vertical plank siding and double-hung windows

INTERIOR: Living/dining room, kitchen, three bedrooms

1948 ADDITION: Garage and workshop

1952 ADDITION: Guestroom and greenhouse

1957 ADDITION: Storage to the garage

1960 REMODELING: Modernized the kitchen

FRONTAGE: 110 feet, lot #11 of Glenwood Subdivision

MAP LOCATION: G4, not numbered

FOLKERS COTTAGE

Dr. Leonard and Fern (Roelf) Folkers were friends of Wallace and Jessie Charters from Stevens College in Columbia, Missouri, where he was Director of Student Health. They stayed at Tom House's cottages one year and liked it so much the decided to build. They purchased just to the west of the Glen Lake Yacht Club and had Harford Field design a cottage which included an office and two bedrooms. It was built in 1952 by John Hatlem.

Cheney Log Cottage

(Cheney Family Collection)

The oldest of six children, Calvin Cheney worked as a lumberjack and on his father's farm in Hart, Michigan. As a young newlywed he was lured away by an offer of $45 a month to manage an apple orchard on Miller Hill known as Chicago Canning. This began his career in 1911 as a manager of fruit operations and farm associations, a career that would take him to Empire, Traverse City, Grand Rapids, Lapeer and finally Iowa, where he owned two ice cream businesses. He was joined in these travels by his wife Cora (Graff) and their five children. When the Cheney family returned to the Glen Lake area on visits, Calvin bought property for investment. He purchased this property on the south shore of Little Glen in 1926 from Willard Wickham. The family would camp on it in the early 1930s, and Calvin would dream of one day building a log cabin.

In 1941 with the help of Matt Breithaupt and his team of work horses, the Cheneys began felling poplar logs on their property. Cora dutifully stripped the bark off the logs, while John Hatlem helped build the log home. Facing scarce building materials during World War II, Cheney salvaged materials from his ice cream company. Construction, which took place during vacations, was completed in 1945. An entrance and half bedroom were added to the back during construction. The stonemason meticulously matched sizes and coloring of the cut granite, transported from Cheney's hometown of Hart, for the fireplace. Lake Leelanau fieldstones on the chimney wall line a hallway leading to the bedroom. Oak flooring is laid at angles radiating from the edge of the fireplace.

Cheney also built a six-stall boathouse with a workshop where he spent many hours. His friend and neighbor John Lorenz, owner of Lorenz Buick in Lansing, Michigan, kept his boat in the boathouse. It is reported that Cheney always drove Buicks and once traded Lorenz a nearby lot for a new Buick. Cheney retired to this much beloved area in the mid-1950s. The cottage remains in the family virtually unchanged.

Cheney family camping on their property in 1930 *(Cheney Family Collection)*

1941 Matt Breithaupt on left and Calvin Cheney on right *(Cheney Family Collection)*

Cheney boathouse construction *(Cheney Family Collection)*

1945

CALVIN AND CORA CHENEY
LOG COTTAGE

BUILDER: Calvin Cheney and John Hatlem, Burdickville, Michigan

COTTAGE: Poplar full-log structure, 40' x 27' in plan

INTERIOR: Living/dining room with oak floors and granite-block fireplace, kitchen, 1½ bedrooms, attic bedroom and storage reached by a pull-down staircase

OUTBUILDINGS: Two-car garage with guest quarters and hot water furnace, six-stall boathouse/workshop no longer exists

FRONTAGE: 200 feet

MAP LOCATION: 8C, not numbered

Koch Cottage *(Lygeo Lodge)*

George F. Koch, Jr. owned Koch-Doerrie Studios, an interior design firm in Cincinnati, Ohio, and his wife Lysle (Drake) worked with him. They were introduced to Glen Lake by his brother John who had visited the area to fish with his friend Verne Harris. George and Lysle began renting a cottage in the mid-1940s from Joseph and Mabel Paulin who owned a grocery store in Burdickville and rented four cottages behind the store on Glen Lake. The Kochs had two children, George F. III, and Robert. In 1949, their 15-year-old nephew John McCormick came to live with the Kochs after his parents Lillian (Koch) and Orville had passed away.

In 1948 the Kochs purchased lake frontage on Dunn's Farm Road, north of Old Settlers Park, from the Paulins for $25 a front foot. The following year, they built a pre-fabricated Braun Cedar Cabin of vertical logs, the Menominee model, and named it *Lygeo Lodge*, after themselves. The cedar logs for the 28' x 22' cottage with an 8' x 16' screened porch were cut and seasoned in Canada and shipped via the Detroit River on the historic schooner, the *J. T. Wing*, to the Braun Lumber Company. The logs were then milled and assembled into kits containing everything needed for assembly on site. The unassembled two-bedroom cabin with loft was delivered on two trucks. The family stayed in

tents during the initial construction and kept their perishables cool in a covered box in the spring on their property.

When George's sister Freda and her husband Richard Flerlage came to visit in 1951, they also fell in love with Glen Lake, purchased property and built a Bellaire log kit cottage, also photographed in this book, in Burdickville. Both families vacationed in their cottage in summers and often during Thanksgiving and Christmas.

The two Braun cottages remain in original condition and are owned and rented out by the family.

In addition to the *Lygeo Lodge*, in 1955 the Kochs built a second Braun Cabin, a one-bedroom reversed Algonac model, which measured 20' x 16' with an 8' x 10' porch. The kit cost $2380.71. The itemized invoice included 90 separate items for a total of 2800 pieces, including double-sided flooring, rustic railings, finished screens, 109 pounds of nails and caulk.

1949

George and Lysle Koch Cottage
(Lygeo Lodge)

Builder: 1949 Harold Weinert,
Lake Leelanau, Michigan

1955 John Hatlem, Burdickville, and
Charles Musil, Glen Arbor, Michigan

Cottage: Braun Menominee model cedar groove and spline log cottage kit; two cut and whole fieldstone chimneys

Interior: Living room with loft, kitchen, two bedrooms

1955: Braun Algonac model three-room cedar log cottage kit

Outbuildings: 1950 Braun cedar log garage kit

Frontage: 100 feet

Map Location: L8, not numbered

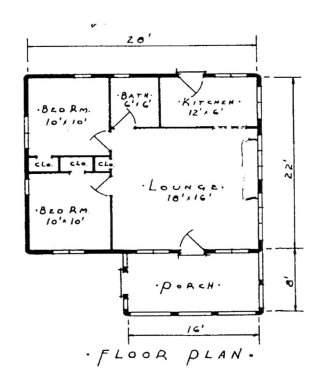

· FLOOR PLAN ·

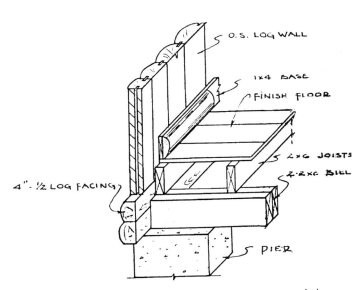

VERTICAL SECTION THROUGH OUTSIDE WALL

FLERLAGE LOG COTTAGE *(Driftwood)*

Dick and Freda Flerlage brought their family north to Glen Lake from Cincinnati, Ohio, in 1951. Freda's brother John Koch had begun camping in the area in the 1940s. He was soon followed by another brother, George, who bought land and built a log cabin in Burdickville just north of Old Settlers Picnic Grounds in 1947. That cottage, which is also included in this book, is named *Lygeo Lodge* and remains in the family. After considerable coaxing on George's part, Freda and Dick came to the lake for a visit. Although Dick would later confess to having complained considerably about the 500-mile drive and the "middle of nowhere" destination, Glen Lake soon worked its magic on both him and Freda. In short order they were looking for a place of their own and later that year acquired a parcel on the south shore of Glen Lake, on the former site of the County Poor House in Burdickville.

In 1953 Dick contracted with the Bellaire Log Cabin Manufacturing Company in Bellaire, Michigan, to have a two-bedroom log cottage and matching boathouse built on the property. All of the necessary components arrived at the site ready to be assembled. After construction began, there were difficulties with the out-of-town firm hired to build the cabin and Dick turned to local craftsmen John and Fred Lanham to complete the job satisfactorily. John Lanham continued to maintain the property for the next 25 years and the Lanham and Flerlage families became close friends. Much of the furniture was made by hand at Dick Flerlage's marine business in Cincinnati.

Being of a somewhat meticulous nature, Dick occasionally considered replacing the rustic cabin with a more substantial home, but the rest of the family's love for the Bellaire kit house always won out. The Flerlage's cottage, named *Driftwood*, remains in the family with both exterior and interior virtually unchanged from the day it was completed over 50 years ago.

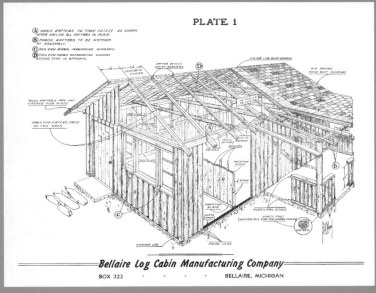

PLATE 1

Ⓐ NOTCH RAFTERS TO TAKE FRIEZE AS SHOWN
AFTER NAILING ALL RAFTERS IN PLACE.
Ⓑ PORCH RAFTERS TO BE NOTCHED
AT ASSEMBLY.
Ⓒ THIS VIEW SHOWS INSWINGING WINDOWS.
Ⓓ THIS VIEW SHOWS OUTSWINGING WINDOW
EITHER TYPE IS OPTIONAL.

Bellaire Log Cabin Manufacturing Company

BOX 322 · BELLAIRE, MICHIGAN

1953

DICK AND FREDA FLERLAGE LOG COTTAGE
(Driftwood)

BUILDER: John and Fred Lanham
COTTAGE: One-story Bellaire cedar vertical
tongue-and-groove half-log cottage,
fieldstone chimney, shingled roof with
rolled edge
INTERIOR: Living room/dining with split-
stone fireplace, kitchen, front porch, two
bedrooms with open loft sleeping area above
OUTBUILDING: Bellaire cedar log kit
boathouse with rolled-edge shingled roof
MAP LOCATION: J10, not numbered

SMOCK COTTAGE

In 1965, Dr. Sidney N. and Ann Smock were introduced to the north shore of Little Glen Lake by their friends Julius and Sally Johnson who summered here. The Smocks subsequently purchased two nearby lots that were owned by the Pierce Stocking family.

While living in Midland, Michigan, the Smocks had rented several homes designed by architects Alden B. Dow and Jackson B. Hallett, who left Dow's employ to form his own architectural firm. The Smocks hired Hallett to design their cottage. Possessing boundless energy and enthusiasm, Hallett spent many hours on the shore visualizing the final design. It is an unusual and spectacularly designed cottage based on a triangular module with interior angles of either 60 or 120 degrees to provide optimal lake views. The design for this cottage won Hallett the First Honor Award from the American Institute of Architects in 1967.

1965

Dr. Sidney N. and Ann Smock Cottage

Architect: Jackson B. Hallett, Midland, Michigan

Builders: Ken Kieft and John Dorsey, Glen Arbor, Michigan

Exterior: Two-story contemporary design utilizing Onaway stone walls, cedar siding and fir decking

Interior: Cedar siding on walls, fir for window frames, cabinetry and ceilings; stone fireplace with sunken hearth in living room, galley kitchen, downstairs master bedroom and three upstairs bedrooms

1985 Addition: Hallett design added first floor dining room and second floor master bedroom

1998 Addition: Garage designed by Norman Kline, Traverse City architect and Hallett's long-time friend and collaborator, using a triangular module, cedar siding and Onaway stone.

Frontage: 200 feet

Map Location: G6, not numbered

During construction, Dr. Smock paid close attention to all details. He personally cleared the building site, and in the process flattened a borrowed truck with a felled tree. As built, the fireplace was not satisfactory and he ordered it rebuilt to his specifications. The original contractor had difficulty with the non-rectangular design and was replaced by Kieft and Dorsey of Glen Arbor.

Exterior elements are cedar siding, fir decking and Onaway stone laid in an irregular pattern with raked joints. Interior walls are also of cedar siding. Fir is used for the ceilings on the first level, for window frames and the cabinetry. A free-standing Onaway stone fireplace with a six-foot wide sunken hearth is the focal point of the living room. An upper deck walkway, resting on triangular stone piers, extends 50-feet lakeward providing spectacular views of the Sleeping Bear Dunes.

In 1977 the Smocks sold the cottage to their friends, Dr. Ron and Mary VandenBelt, from Ann Arbor. In 1996 George and Carol Quarderer, who knew Jack Hallett in Midland, became the present owners. The cottage has been remodeled twice, but the integrity of the original design has been preserved.

MEMORIES LIVE ON

This is an earlier view from my window on the south shore of Glen Lake. The trees have grown over the years and now we do not see much of the lake. The bridges and trout are gone but the spring-fed pond remains, along with the pump house and the boathouse on what was originally the 1920 Meurer Estate. Eugene Meurer, founder of Muskegon's Central Paper Company, and his wife Margaretha built a cottage with an open plan and large front porch. By the 1950s it was known as Red Rooster Cottages and owned by Roland and Dorothy Clark. It had five rental cottages and loyal renters who loved Glen Lake, some of whom built cottages of their own. My husband Frank and I had sought an old cottage when we decided to move to Glen Lake year-round in 1989, but could not find one. By this time, the original Meurer Cottage had been torn down and replaced. Frank was quietly relieved not to have taken on its maintenance and we were both content with the beauty of the setting. We purchased the property after the first day we saw it, moved up here year-round, enrolled our children in Glen Lake School and have never looked back.

One reason for our move from our beloved Victorian home in Hinsdale, Illinois, was the changes that we saw happening, as smaller bungalows and stately Victorians were razed to make way for larger newly constructed homes that we felt dramatically changed the character of that community. Shortly after our move here, the same

phenomena began to happen around the lake. Charming cottages were being taken down and replaced with large new homes which no longer resembled the old summer lake cottages. We had remodeled the 1970s home on our property but were unable to successfully capture the old cottage charm.

I found myself still longing for an old cottage and searched for one that could be moved to become the home of my bookstore in Glen Arbor. Giving up, I had architectural plans drawn up for a replica of a U.S. Life-Saving Station. When an original early 1920s cedar log cottage from the north shore of Glen Lake was offered, it was an easy decision. It was joyful seeing it arrive in 1998 with flowers still in the window boxes. It has been a perfect structure for the bookstore.

We purchased the cottage from Anne (Stone) and Bruce Lichliter who had been married in front of its fieldstone fireplace. They wanted to build a larger year-round home and the cottage sat in the center of their two lots. Anne's parents, George, a classical music radio host, and Helen Stone had purchased the cottage in the late 1960s after renting from Walter Smith, the previous cottage owner. The Dengs had also rented it. Once a renter stopped in the bookshop and related the story of his father being a conscientious renter who wanted to be allowed to rent again. He picked up all of the Navaho rugs to protect them, but not before drawing the scheme of how to set them back upon leaving. The cottage was originally built

Dr. and Mrs. Lawrence Day   (Dillon Family Collection)

by Dr. and Mrs. Lawrence Day, a doctor in Detroit. Lawrence Day's father was D.H. Day's younger brother Bob, who built the *Lorelei Lodge*, a log cottage that no longer stands on the north shore of Little Glen. Dr. Day spent his honeymoon on Glen Lake and later stayed at Krull's resort and purchased adjacent land from them. After living in the log cottage for awhile, Days decided to build a much enlarged version of this first log cottage further to the west on Sunset Drive.

Upon making our home on Glen Lake, I wanted to learn more about Glen Lake's summer resort history and began recording oral interviews. It was soon clear that lake vacations are vividly remembered with deep warm feelings. I began to dream of finding a photographer with a large format view camera who would be interested in capturing the cottages' interiors. Serendipity arrived when Dietrich Floeter walked into the bookstore. After chatting, it became clear that he was the one to make it all come together and he graciously signed onto the project. His photographs have exceeded my expectations and it has been a pleasure accompanying him on all of the shoots. His photographs are classics in the field of cottage photography. My feeling of loss about never having seen the Meurer cottage has been more than replaced by having had the rare experience of taking in the beauty of these cottages.

It has been easy for all of us who worked on this book to have fallen in love with each cottage. Stories have been graciously shared about their history. They are models for preserving the summer lake family cottage and keeping its memories alive. Dietrich and I hope you are pleased with the results so beautifully pulled together by book designers Angela and Erik Saxon of Saxon Design. They managed to delightfully get us to press on time. Lou Heiser consulted and added his wonderful cottage illustrations. Luckily for all concerned, the text was carefully edited by Linda Young and proofed by Hope Laitala, Marilyn Warburton, and Cynthia Dougal.

I wish to thank everyone who has been a part of this project. My consultants have been Kathryn Eckert, Lou Heiser, Chris Byron and Tom Wilson, Mary Ellen Hadjisky, Kimberly Mann, Dave Taghon, Grace Dickinson, George Weeks, and Laura Quackenbush. Paul Chalup researched cottage ownership in Leland.

Locating the existence of these cottages, their owners and early history has only been accomplished through the assistance of Glen Lake residents and friends who seemingly never tired of my probing questions. Those particularly coming to mind are Bobbi Collins, Web Cook, John Dorsey, Cynthia Dougal, Pat Dutmers, Edwin and Frank Fisher, Tom Flerlage, Sue Frank, Joanne Sprouse, Barbara, Dick and George Schilling, Jeanette Wepking, Nate Whiteside and Bob Worthington.

I would also like to thank over 75 interviewees I have taped since 2001 and those who so ably assisted with taping, indexing and transcribing: Sarah Litch, Shirley Hoagland, Chase Edwards, Sarah Cook, Kimberly Mann, and Codi Yeager. I have also had access to interviews conducted by Chris Wright, Lucille Faulman, Dotti Lanham, Tom Van Zoeren and the Glen Arbor History Group.

Finally, without my daughter Brita's early editorial assistance and my husband Frank's support of my intense devotion to this project, none of this could have been accomplished.

In sincere appreciation, *Barbara Siepker*

BIBLIOGRAPHY

Byron, M. Christine and Thomas R. Wilson, *Vintage Views of Leelanau County*. Chelsea, MI: Sleeping Bear Press, 2002.

Fetzer, Margaret S., *Now and Then*. Self-published, 1973.

Fisher, Edwin L., *Saw Mills and Family Trees: A Fisher Family History and Genealogy*. Self-published, 2006.

Mitchell, John, *Wood Boats of Leelanau: A Photographic Journal*. Leland: Leelanau Historical Museum, 2007.

Rader, Robert Dwight, *Beautiful Glen Arbor Township*. Village Press, 1977.

Schilling, George T., *Looking Back: A Family History and Memoir*. Self-published, 2006.

Scott, Ken and Jerry Dennis, *Leelanau*. Charlevoix: Petunia Press, 2000.

Tozer, James R., *Glen Arbor Pioneers*. Glen Arbor: Leelanau Press, 2003.

Weeks, George, *Sleeping Bear: Yesterday and Today, 2nd* Edition. Ann Arbor: University of Michigan Press, 2005.

Weese, Harry E., *From Bull Creek to Barrington*. Self-published, 1952.

Weese, Kitty Baldwin, *Harry Weese Houses*. Chicago: Chicago Review Press, 1987.

PERIODICALS AND PAMPHLETS

Dickenson, Julia, *Leelanau Enterprise*, August 18, 1966.

"Glen Lake the Most Beautiful Lake in Nation," *Traverse City Record Eagle*, July 31, 1926.

Williams, Maynard Owen, "By Car and Steamer Around Our Inland Seas," *National Geographic Magazine*, April, 1934.

Beauty Spots in Leelanau, 1901 Souvenir. Northport: W.W. Campbell, 1901.

Day, D.H., *Glen Lake Region*. Traverse City: Herald and Record Company, 1911.

Glen Lake, Leelanau County, Michigan: One of the Five Most Beautiful Lakes in the World. Traverse City: L.R. Henderson, 1931.

Grand Traverse Region. Traverse City: Herald Record Company, 1911.

Leelanau County, The Land of Delight. Leland: Leelanau County Board of Supervisors, 1924.

ADDITIONAL RESOURCES

75 oral interviews conducted by the author, private and public postcard and photograph collections, emails and correspondence were used with permission.

Individual cottage information obtained from the following:

Barton Cottage: Cynthia (Barton) Dougal and Wilfrid Barton

Bray Cottage: Kathleen Wiesen and Grace Dickinson

Burr·Pratt Cottage: Bill Pratt and Suzanne Pratt

Casparis Cottage: Peggy (Casparis) Groos

Cheney Cottage: Helen (Heidel) Campbell

Collings·Simpson/Dunscombe Cottage: John "Bart" Collings and Billie (Dunscombe) Kremer

Dean Cottage: Patricia (Dean) Rockwood and Howard Dean

Dickinson Cottage: Grace (Dickinson) Johnson, permission granted to include 1943 map

Dillon Cottage: Ananda (Dillon) Bricker and Barrie (Dillon) Riday

Dunbar·Batchelder·Williams Cottage: Anne Williams and Dr. Bruce Greenfield

Evelyn's Cottage: Ronald Fornowski and Norma Durkee.

Fetzer Cottage: Mary Jane (Fetzer) Bryant and John H. (Jack) Sherman

Field Cottage: Harford Field, Jr., Barbara (Folkers) Astley, Jay Meaden

Fisher·House Cottage: Frank Fisher, Janet (House) Lanthy, Martha (Van Vleck) Pierce, Jerry Conroy, Chuck Kraus

Flerlage Cottage: Tom Flerlage

Fralick Cottage: Karen (Krueger) Ford and Jack Barratt

Glen Lake Yacht Club: Kay (Hench) Whitney, Lillis (Lanphier) Lyon, Nate Whiteside

Gommesen Cottage: Trann (Gommesen) Kelly, Jim Patterson, Barbara Kelly, permission granted for use of circa 1939 map

Goodnow·Brady Cottage: Jennifer Glassman and Barbara Collins

Haggarty Cottage: Richard Schilling and Ann (Haggarty) Warren

Harris Cottage: Betty Rhoades, John Lockwood, Dorothy Draheim

Miller House garage

Hartmann Cottage: John and Shirley Peters, Kanitz familly

Hench·Symonds Cottage: Roswell Jennings, Nathaniel Marshall Symonds, Scott Jones

Hoblet·Dennison Cottage: H.H. Cobb, Jr., Barbara (Whiteside) Schilling, Scott Jones

Johnson Cottage: Yvonne Daly and Francis Baad

Jones Cottage: Gary Jones

Keen·Mercer Cottage: Gay (Mercer) Budinger, Bobbi (Keen) Collins, Ann (Wright) Davey

Koch Cottage: John McCormick

Lanphier Cottage: Kathryn (Lanphier) Wangren and Robert Carr Lanphier

Lerchen Cottage: Richard Green and William Dotterweich

Lewis Cottage: Anton DuPont and Marilyn Johnson

Lott Cottage: William and Karen Lott, Bev and Wade Fetzer

Miller House: Miller family history from Empire Area History Museum and Bill Martin

Peppler Cottage: Linda and John Peppler

Raines Cottage: Robert and John Raines, Mary Rodman, Barbara (Whiteside) Schilling

Rea·Whiteside Cottage: Barbara (Whiteside) Schilling and Nate Whiteside

Robinson Cottage: Charles Robinson

Rohr·Zelle Cottage: Anne Zelle and family

Sherwood Shack: Web Cook

Smock Cottage: George Quarderer

Spouse Cottage: Joanne L. Sprouse and George A. Vogel

Stearns Cottage: Lois J. (Stearns) Swierad

Walker House: Robert W. Nissen

Warren·Senter Cottage: Robin McKenna and Laurel Jeris

Weese Cottages: Sue (Weese) Frank and Ben Weese

Wells Cottage: Sue Danielson and family, Dan and Magee Gordon

White·Schilling Cottage: George T. and Barbara (White) Schilling

Wilson Cottage: Mary Jane (Fetzer) Bryant, John H. (Jack) Sherman, Mary (Sherman) Mortimer

Worthington Cottage: Robert W. Worthington

Pritchard Cottage

INDEX